*When all that stands
between death and freedom
is a ride...*

Ike was adopted from the Lab Rescue Of L.R.C.P. Inc., in Oakton, Virginia.
Photo by Kelly Whaley

Fifteen Legs

*When all that stands
between death and freedom
is a ride...*

by Bonnie Silva

RIVERBANK PRESS
Yorktown, Virginia

First Edition
10 9 8 7 6 5 4 3 2 1

Published by Riverbank Press
311 Jethro Lane, Yorktown, Virginia 23692
www.riverbankpress.com

Book design by Saxon Design, Inc.
Traverse City, Michigan
Printed in the USA
Cover photo by Kelly Whaley: Maya is a Lab mix rescued by Coastal Animal Hospital
in Savannah, Georgia.

Library of Congress Control Number is available from the publisher
Silva, Bonnie
  Fifteen Legs: When all that stands between death and freedom is a ride/Bonnie Silva
  ISBN 978-0-9728991-1-6
1. Pets 2. Animals

A portion of all proceeds from this book will be donated to animal shelters
and rescue groups.

This book is available at special discounts when purchased in quantities for use in
fund-raising and education purposes. For details, contact Riverbank Press.

Dedication

This book is dedicated to Bailey
and to Walker, each of whom traveled
fifteen legs to their adoptive homes.

Bailey, a senior Miniature Poodle,
was rescued from a kill-shelter in
Ohio and traveled to Colorado.
He was renamed Mortie, and
died just a few weeks after being
welcomed into Ellen's loving arms.

Walker, a young black Aussie-mix,
was rescued from a county pound in
North Carolina and traveled to New
England. The former pound puppy
is now a much-loved member of the
Squatrito family. I'm told he dances
and rejoices every time it snows…

Kittens await adoption at the Heritage Humane Society in Williamsburg, Virginia.

*We can judge the heart of a man
by his treatment of animals.*

Immanual Kant

Contents

Prologue

It always hurts to have a door slammed in my face, but like Wile E. Coyote, I usually manage to somehow get peeled off the door's surface and move on.

Such was the case when I shared the concept for *Fifteen Legs* with a potential filmmaking partner. "It's just not of sufficient social significance," he said unapologetically and all in one breath. His response when translated from industry speak meant simply, "No thanks, no one cares about that."

I believed otherwise but didn't beg to differ with him. I didn't even bother to ask him if he could repeat his tongue twister of a reply three times fast.

This notion of volunteers connecting in cyberspace on behalf of desperate, unwanted animals had stolen my heart. The thought of perfect strangers coming together and working as a team to shuttle society's non-human cast-offs out of harm's way was too wonderful a story to pass up. I had to tell it.

I had already signed myself up to serve as this project's producer, and there was no turning back. Though he didn't know it yet, I had also enlisted Russ, my fiancé, to direct and edit the show.

Everywhere I went I asked people if they were aware of this incredible cyber-based railroad used to move homeless animals all over the map, sometimes only hours before their lives were to be permanently snuffed out. Almost no one had heard of the volunteer animal transport system, but almost everyone, upon learning about it, became excited and asked how they personally could get involved.

It was a clammy day in August when I read Eve Haslam's article "Godspeed to All Those in Transport" and within a few minutes, I had soaked the newsprint with tears. There was a dog, a black Lab, who needed to get from her foster home in Georgia to her adoptive home in Vermont. She was put on a "transport" and handed off to different volunteer drivers, fifteen in all, until finally she arrived where her new family was waiting – the dog's "forever home," as the animal-people called it.

"If only I had known about this animal rescue and transport thing," I thought as I laid the newspaper aside. "I could have...I would have known how to...I would have been able to, to somehow...."

I wanted to write about it, but I couldn't. For now, my emotions had me under arrest, tormenting me with what might have been, if only I had known.

My decision to enter the world of animal rescue and transport through a camera's eye was not the result of reading one article, or learning of one dog's plight. Something inside me had already been brewing for just the right amount of time: when the last few ingredients were tossed in, the mixture couldn't just simmer anymore; it bubbled up and boiled over onto a page.

One of the last items to go into my pot of thoughts was in an issue of my daughter's *Weekly Reader*. The cover grabbed my attention with the face of a chimpanzee and the caption: *"Do Animals Have Feelings?"* Pondering how poorly we had fared as a species to be posing this question at all, I looked inside. Scientists cited examples of animals experiencing human feelings like love and grief. The writer then added something I didn't expect to find at our date in history, in a publication used widely as a learning tool for kids.

"Other scientists doubt that chimps, rodents, and other mammals have humanlike feelings. They argue that people tend to see human qualities in animals. That's why whales seem to show signs of being in love, or dogs seem to be sad, they say...Many scientists also argue that no scientific way to determine whether animals have emotions exists yet."[1]

Soon afterward, I attended a lecture by Jane Goodall and as she looked out over the crowd and bellowed hope in her rendition of a chimp's howl, I caught her reverberations and added them to my soup.

As I was gearing up for what would be the ride of my life, Sam Patton, the best camera operator I know, came forward and offered his support. The crew now numbered three, and little did I know how quickly that number would escalate, or how people would give of themselves so generously for the animals needing their help.

So off we went, packed with our broadcast equipment and wide-open minds. Also in the bag were great expectations, a notebook filled with questions, and some hearts that we wore on our sleeves.

Tucked into one of my pockets was a tiny jar of skepticism containing a note from an experienced animal rescuer. Her admonition, "Ninety percent of people who rescue animals belong to a subculture who hate people," was delivered self-assuredly, in a "You'll see…" kind of way. Still, I was exhilarated. We had committed to a fascinating project, and we were on our way.

This is the story of animals who have run out of time. It's about the people who save them at the eleventh hour. It's the story of where they go next, and how they get there.

---

[1] "Do Animals Have Feelings?" *Weekly Reader*, Senior Edition, January 5, 2001.

Our Pet
Overpopulation Problem

The Humane Society of the United States tells us that according to their estimates, 6-8 million homeless dogs and cats enter the shelter system every year.* They also estimate that 3-4 million of these cats and dogs are adopted. A small percentage (15-30% of dogs and 2-5% of cats) who end up in shelters are reclaimed by their caregivers. The remaining 3-4 million dogs and cats are not adopted, and therefore they do not leave the shelter. They are euthanized.

Two unspayed/unneutered animals = lots more animals.

If the average female dog can produce 2 litters of puppies per year with 6-10 puppies in each litter, then in just six years, she and her offspring could theoretically produce 67,000 dogs. The average female cat can produce 3 litters per year with an average of 4-6 kittens per litter. In seven years, one female cat and her offspring could theoretically produce 420,000 cats.

*Many homeless animal advocates believe this number to be far greater.
(Stat. Source: HSUS, Updated Oct. 12, 2006)

Our Puppy Mill Problem

Though at least 3-4 million cats and dogs are euthanized every year, people continue to purchase puppies from pet stores, online venues, and classified ads. Many of these animals come from puppy mills, cruel operations where puppies are produced as commodities while their parents endure miserable lives. The conditions animals are forced to bear in these facilities are no longer secret, so it is no surprise to learn that the resultant puppies often have genetic defects, serious illnesses, and behavior problems.

People who purchase milled puppies are often unprepared to cope with what comes next. They find themselves living with an animal produced the cheapest way possible, without regard to genetic traits, physical condition, and other factors critical for producing sound, healthy puppies. Before long, many of these animals make their way into the shelter system, where they have little if any chance of being adopted.

Chapter One
SHELTERS

The word "shelter," as it is used in reference to the many buildings across the country where homeless animals are housed, presents a grave and troubling contradiction for me. Prior to working on this project, I associated the word "shelter" with places of safety. When I heard someone speak of this or that shelter, I imagined protective havens and sanctuaries of all types, where people and non-humans could take refuge if they had nowhere else to be. The research required to put this story together exposed my own ignorance of a very present and ugly reality, and my previously held notions of shelters, specifically animal shelters, were shattered.

Kill Versus No-Kill

In the world of animal rescue and transport, volunteers use the terms "kill-shelter" and "no-kill shelter" to differentiate between which shelters routinely euthanize animals to create space for incoming homeless animals, and which ones do not. Some people take issue with the term "kill-shelter" – asserting that this terminology unfairly indicts individuals who participate in the grim task of euthanizing completely adoptable animals. But even a softer term like "euthanizing-shelter," if it were to be used, cannot provide a thick enough gloss to conceal the disturbing, awful truth.

Animals who are euthanized or "put to sleep" do not wake up, ever. Whether they are euthanized by lethal injection, gassed or destroyed by other unspeakable means, they are no longer with us when the process of euthanizing them is complete. They cease to eat, drink, cry, bark, meow, play and feel. They are gone.

Left Behind

For many animals, their troubles begin and end when they are brought or "surrendered" to a shelter. Lorraine Ehrhart and her group of doting volunteers regularly engage in the head-banging and hoop-jumping necessary to spare the lives of approximately sixty animals a month from Miami's Animal Services facility.

When asked why animals are surrendered, Lorraine's frustration with anyone who would purposefully leave an animal behind eventually gave way to profound sadness.

We have heard every reason in the book for an animal to be surrendered to the shelter...

"The animal has brown fur and I've bought a white couch and he sheds, and he doesn't match the furniture anymore."

There was a woman surrendering a little dog, a little female dog, cute as can be, and I said, "Why are you giving this dog up?" And she said, "She's in heat." And I tried to explain to her that there's something you can do about that, but no, she was in heat...

Very often it's: "We're moving, we can't take the dog."

"The dog got too big, we liked it when it was a puppy."

"We're getting a divorce."

Sometimes it's just sheer hatred at the other spouse. They'll come and take the dog and dump it at the shelter, just to get back at a spouse.

Some people will have an older dog. The dog's not feeling well, so they take it to the vet, and the vet says this dog has cancer or this dog has some disease that's expensive to treat, so instead of treating it, they take it to the shelter.

The reasons are far flung. But people don't realize what happens to their animal when it goes to the shelter. I've heard people say "Oh no, they're gonna find a home," (for this big black mutt) and it's just not going to happen.

The true story is that when the animal comes in, they're processed and put in a kennel, and held. If it's a stray, the dog is held for six days, waiting for the owner to come. If it's an owner-surrender, there's no mandatory holding period for that dog.

Shelter dog #B2

The vast majority of them are not adopted, and they get sick. They're missing their family, they're sick, they're scared, they're hungry because they won't eat because they're so stressed — and then they end up on the euthanasia table and they get put to sleep.

For the vast majority of dogs and cats, that's what happens to them.

Lorraine Ehrhart, Director
Miami-Dade Rescue Railroad

I don't think I could have really understood the need for animal transport until I fully grasped the gravity of the situations these animals face. My learning curve was agonizing. It forced me to be privy to information such as which animals were out of time and the dates they would be unwittingly put to sleep. One click, and they were all looking at me.

```
[OnTheRoadAgain] NY - Dogs - This is the euth.
list for Sunday. Please help...
```

I learned early on that homeless animals are not in danger because monsters loom and lie in wait to kill them when their shelter stay expires. Their lives are in peril because there is not enough room for them, and because our society currently allows homeless animals to be destroyed and disposed of when the space they inhabit is required for yet another unwanted, unfortunate creature.

For Lorraine, Debbie, Gayle, Kevin, Sandy, Stacy, Kara, Cynthia, Janet, Rande, and the many other people I have been so privileged to know, this modus operandi is simply unacceptable; and even more so they say, if we dare call ourselves a modern and civilized society.

I thought about the creatures hopelessly trapped in society's unwanted animal web and mulled over what could be done for them. The truth was depressing. So far, the solutions I've heard proposed to end or even lessen this problem require an enormous shift in the way we perceive and respond to our nation's homeless animals. Even if society crawls out of the dark and eventually reaches that elusive tipping point – the spark that will finally ignite and alter our mindset and behavior – it will be too late for millions of homeless animals. Not hundreds. Not thousands. Millions.

The aforementioned people have made conscious decisions to move beyond the bleak details in favor of doing something, no matter how small, to alleviate animal homelessness and its associated miseries wherever they may find it.

In the eyes of these seemingly ordinary yet quite extraordinary individuals, each number coming up for euthanasia corresponds to a tag. Each tag is attached to a living being with fur, a tail, and a face that begs to be loved. Each life at risk necessitates swift action on the part of a team of people who know how to work together to get things done.

Seize The Day!

For people positioned on the front lines of homeless animal life saving, there is *today* to contend with, and if today there is one heartworm-positive Beagle and three tabby kittens at death's door, then there is no time to rant, rave, theorize or place blame. A rescue is in order, and though it can't as yet solve all of our homeless animal woes, technology will be summoned to do some wonderful and awe-inspiring things.

Re: [OnTheRoadAgain] please notice, we have a chicken to rescue …

Re: MDRR Sharpei with chain embedded in neck

[masscats*] Best Friends Animal Society Enters St. Bernard Parish
*masscats is a Yahoo group in MA that helps homeless felines

[NMHP] Tippy, The Ugly Pup-ling

[OnTheRoadAgain] I NEED HELP!! "Katrina" Horse Relief Effort

[OnTheRoadAgain] Bunny Transport: Fredonia, NY - Little Rock, AR, Sept. 24-25

MDRR Miami - Beautiful Labs Languishing at Shelter

[TRUCK-N-PAWS] This transport is filled!

[OnTheRoadAgain] Huskies in Baton Rouge … URGENT

MDRR Super Pull Saturday

[CARescueRR] Fwd: Irish Wolfhound in Agoura shelter since Aug.

Re: MDRR Border Collies Getting Sprung - With Your Help

Chapter Two
TECHNOLOGY

It's the way rescue and transport is done...

The road most homeless animals travel is a dead end,
but for some, a miracle is only an email away.

Although this line would eventually make its way into the
production's tease, I never liked it. Yes, it surely sounded like tease
material when it was delivered as a voice-over segment, but the word
"some" bothered me. I was falling in love with society's non-human
cast-offs and, believing that they were all deserving, I wanted technology to help deliver a miracle for every homeless animal – not for
just a few.

Our crew would soon be taking a seat alongside these lucky
animals and their devoted escorts and, like any producer, I was interested in the back-story. I wanted to know everything about this
incredible yet largely undiscovered railroad.

My investigation points tumbled out all at once and got
scribbled onto recycled paper and crammed into the pocket area of
my notebook:

  ✦ So where in cyberspace did animal-people get together? How
    did they find out about the animals' departure and arrival dates?
    What kinds of people volunteer to drive rescued creatures
    from one place to another, and why do they do it?

  ✦ Who organizes and manages these rescued-animal journeys,
    or do things just sort of fall into place? Do the furry passen-

gers ever get animal-knapped along the way by ill-intentioned people posing as transporters?

+ Is this transport thing some kind of a clandestine club comprised of people I would never want to take to lunch, or can anyone join? Is it legal to shuffle animals from state to state, or does the transporting of animals across state lines help to spread disease?

+ Is such an elaborate and time-consuming network really necessary? Is it effective? Why don't the adopters just pay to fly these rescued animals home? What about the misunderstood dog breeds that some people are afraid of – are they allowed to ride?

Like an adult in a six-year-old's skin, I was bursting with curiosity. There was just so much that intrigued me about how, with the aid of technology, these animals could literally go from being dangerously out of time to having wonderfully pampered lives, sometimes in only a matter of days.

Two generous and experienced volunteers were kind enough to put up with me during what I call my "Animal Transport 101" phase. One of these women, Debbie Farenholtz, lives in Rhode Island and provided a fitting introduction to my querying.

> Technology plays a very big part in the way that transport systems are set up now to get dogs back and forth. If it weren't for the internet, we wouldn't have that large base of volunteers and we wouldn't have the tools to set up and coordinate the transports.
>
> It's a lot of work to get a dog from Point A to Point B when there's a thousand or two thousand miles to cover, and getting volunteers to cover a hundred miles or fifty miles or two hundred miles of that leg would be hard if you had to do it over the phone or writing letters.
>
> The internet is a great way to do that because we can go onto groups, we can meet up, we can say, "Hey, we've got a dog that we need to get from North Carolina up to

Massachusetts. Who can help? And who can coordinate this? Who can plan us a route?" Who can then jump on and say, "I will drive a hundred miles to take this dog to its new home and get it its freedom and a new life?"

Debbie Fahrenholtz
Puppy Mill Rescue Foster Mom

So okay, I mused. According to Debbie, the internet is an awesome and powerful tool, a conduit for all of the activities required to save homeless animals in trouble.

Sandy Clabaugh, from *Almost Home Dachshund Rescue* seemed eager to share the nuts and bolts of coordinating these trips. She described what it was like to be the one elected to glue the transport team together and set its wheels in motion.

I've been in rescue for four years. I can't imagine how it even was done prior to emails and computers.

It's extremely stressful trying to put a transport together. You have so many legs. You get Mapquest out, you get an atlas out, you see where you start, you see where you're going – you've never been to that part of the country, you have no idea what the towns are like or where the meeting places are.

You start mapping out sixty miles, sixty miles, sixty miles, then you put it all together, you start posting it on the internet, it'll take two weeks, you get all these responses. You sift through them, you put together more emails. It's a royal pain, but it's been responsible for getting these dogs moved.

And I would much rather the dogs move on that type of transport where there's very few dogs moving at one time. They're getting individual attention, they're with people who have done transports before, they know about keeping them safe at roadside park areas, they know about giving them water and food, and the dogs are being spoiled all along the way.

I think that's the least stressful way for the dogs to be transported. You could put them on an airplane, but that's very stressful, so I love the transport system – it's just a pain.

Sandy laughed, leading me to believe she had a love-hate relationship with the business of filling "legs." She made it sound like orchestrating and monitoring the movements of rescued animals in transit can be mentally taxing, and very time consuming.

Generally, you get several people that come in that can help with one leg, but you've got three other legs on each side that nobody can help with, and you have to really go in and start doing some begging, and twisting some arms, and maybe shifting routes.

Areas that are totally dead, nobody comes through, so then you're having to do more emailing to shelters or other places that might be able to put somebody in.

Then you get it all put together and somebody backs out. And if they back out too far down close to the deadline, that can cancel the whole thing.

Then you start rescheduling it, and Sue who could do it last week can't do it next week, so now you're going back and you're digging through emails for other people who volunteered for those legs. It just becomes a major headache there.

Sandy Clabaugh
Almost Home Dachshund Rescue

[TRUCK-N-PAWS] Crosspost Widely: 5 Legs Still Needed VA-WV-PA for Pom

So far, no one had made any of this sound easy, but is anything worthwhile ever easy?

I shuffled through my interview notebook, which was becoming heavier by the day. Eventually, I found what I was looking for: someone had said something about rescued animals knowing that they have been rescued, something about a look of gratitude in their eyes. I wanted to see that look for myself, and decided that even if all of my efforts failed with the documentary, we would capture that look on tape for everyone to see.

Chapter Three
POSTING

Say something good – my life depends on it...

> The internet has just changed rescue completely because now we can take the little faces and put them on the internet and say "Look at this little poodle, and isn't he adorable, and don't you have a perfect home for him in your rescue?"
>
> Lorraine Ehrhart
> Miami-Dade Rescue Railroad (MDRR)

The pleas posted in cyberspace to publicize the needs of homeless animals reverberate with real-life drama. They almost whimper audibly. They are painful to read. Each time I visited the sites featuring these heart-wrenching appeals, I felt as though I was being personally introduced to the six million or more animals still waiting for a home, one at a time.

Once having met Lucy, the two-year-old Golden Retriever on line, and having been made aware that she had only three days left to live, I couldn't easily click away, or allow my screen to darken. I felt somehow accountable to Lucy, somehow responsible for ensuring the worst didn't befall this beautiful, homeless dog.

Thankfully, it was also here in this virtual wonderland that animal lovers surfaced and responded to the messages meant to tug at peoples' hearts.

```
[masscats] Matt was adopted!

MDRR Found rescue for babies

[OnTheRoadAgain] Barney has been rescued
```

A few good people who had heard about our escapades came forward in the early stages of the production to offer a helping hand. Pepper Lindsey, a first-rate producer based in Florida, volunteered to interview Lorraine. I opened Pepper's package expectantly and once the broadcast footage was transferred, I got prepared to log my favorite takes and the corresponding time code numbers.

My excitement soon dissipated. Lorraine's interview footage left me motionless and in an emotionally drained heap on our Southern yellow pine wood floor. I reached for the remote and felt too numb to do much else but turn her off.

"It can't be," I said to myself while wading through my research files. "It just can't be."

"It is," I confirmed as I highlighted the shocking statistics in neon yellow. Grief-stricken over the plight of Miami's homeless animals, I shut down our equipment and went for a walk.

Nature has a way of providing solace, even when our paths are laden with tears. Only God and I know what percolated within me that day among the oak trees. Or perhaps the trees knew too, because their leaves rustled briskly at just the right time, as if urging me to get back to work.

I entered my little studio renewed, and sat squarely in front of the monitor. I took a deep breath, pressed play, and let Lorraine continue.

Miami-Dade Rescue Railroad's focus is on moving animals from Miami-Dade Animal Services to rescue groups capable of finding them a home. This approach buys time for animals who, for many reasons, are not likely to be adopted by the general public.

Lorraine revisited the process of posting the animals – something she and her volunteers do faithfully on the message boards week after week after week…

MDRR UPDATE:] MIAMI - Terrier Mixes/Lots of
Puppies/Schnauzer/Corgi Mix

It's sad, but you don't have that much time, so you try to just post the ones that you think you can get into rescue, that you think the rescues will be able to adopt.

We have to pick and choose, and it's awful, because we only have so much time, we only have so much space, so we have to post the dogs that we think rescues can take.

They're little dogs, because in Miami we have an over-abundance of little purebreed dogs that are being put to sleep every single day.

In other parts of this state, and in other parts of the country, they have waiting lists for small breed dogs – they're crying for small breed dogs in rescue.

In other parts of the country because they have very successful spay and neuter programs, there aren't a lot of stray dogs running around, especially small dogs.

So those are the types of dogs we have to focus on, we're forced to focus on. And the large breed dogs – the dogs that are pure breeds, even purebred German Shepherds – there's just no room for them.

Purebred beautiful yellow Labs, black Labs, there's just no room for big dogs.

So very often we have to turn a blind eye to a dog that is completely adoptable because the other rescue groups just don't have the space for them.

And it's heartbreaking when you see the big black or brown mutt, the-run-of-the-mill Heinz 57 who looks at you with those imploring eyes and the wagging tail, and you have to turn your head.

So the pictures are posted, then the rescue groups hopefully read those posts and let us know which animals

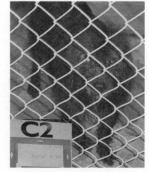

Shelter dog #C2.

they're interested in taking. We put a hold on those animals the next day because we're only given twenty-four hours. We have to get somebody into the shelter to pull the animal out.

Lorraine Ehrhart
Miami-Dade Rescue Railroad

RE: MDRR URGENT: Miami - White GSD
Pregnant Lab Mix/Two Mammas with Babies

I wanted to know what happened to the animals posted on the message boards, but it was becoming hard for me to visit the cyber sites where they lived. The presence of the unwanted faces and their dire circumstances overwhelmed me. It was as if I could feel them drowning in a virtual sea of heartache and despair.

Worst of all, it appeared only a few fortunate creatures would be thrown a life raft in time to save them. And only a very small number in comparison to the total number of animals in shelters would make it out alive.

One of the posts still haunts me. Actually, there were several posts from a man who seemed to be trying to intercept and rescue a large group of Beagles before they were sold. He appeared to be quite distraught over the dogs and pleaded with members for help.

His last distressing post made it all quite clear.

"... Those dirty #@&!!! Those Beagles will never again see the light of day."

Attempts to pay "ransom" for the dogs were unsuccessful, and they were shipped to a research lab.

I logged out of all my groups, and couldn't return to the place where I learned that people experiment on Beagles for a very, very long time.

Chapter Four
TO THE RESCUE...

[OnTheRoadAgain] Fwd: Urgent situation at
Kill shelter (out of room)

Animals, I learned, were in need of being pulled out of shelters for a vast array of reasons. And not all shelter animals were "surrenders." Some were strays existing on their own. Others had been seized by authorities due to abuse or neglect. Many had been lovingly cared for until their guardians became ill or died. Still others had been made homeless by weather. Some animals were simply lost.

I began interviewing people engaged in the unsung and largely unseen love labor known as rescue. Most of these interviewees bravely sweated through a few minutes of camera-induced apprehension, then they were on a roll. After all, the rescuers reminded me, homeless animals were badly in need of the public's help; therefore, they would gladly speak on their behalf no matter how difficult or uncomfortable it was.

I discovered that much of a rescuer's work is done speedily, as there is precious little time to put together and carry out a plan. In many cases, a whole cast of complete strangers collaborates to work out a dizzying mishmash of details before it's too late.

And even in the world of animal rescue, one can specialize. A volunteer's personal interests and talents can be directed toward helping a particular breed, solving a location-specific problem, or becoming involved in a myriad of other rescue-related activities.

Some volunteers had a soft spot for pound puppies; others cared deeply for feral cats. But everyone I spoke with in the world of animal rescue seemed to agree on two fronts: that homeless animals face frightening uncertainties; and an urgent need exists for many more volunteers willing to come to their aid.

Gayle Fitzpatrick and friends.

Over the weeks spent interviewing rescuers, my crew and I exchanged handshakes and best wishes with some very kind and passionate individuals. I also met some animals whose lives had been scarred by people on the other end of what humans are capable of doing.

The dogs loved and cared for by Gayle Fitzpatrick and her trusty volunteers have seen it all.

> *Once a month, sometimes every six weeks, depending on the rate of adoptions for the dogs presently with us, we will bring ten to fifteen dogs up from very high-kill shelters in Georgia and try to find them homes.*
>
> *…We also have people who volunteer their time to drive an hour, pass the dogs off, drive another hour, pass the dogs off.*
>
> *…A lot of times there's no place for those dogs to go. If they're not pulled out of that shelter immediately, then they're never going to get out. So there has to be some type of system of volunteers willing to do this and they're all over the country, and it's truly amazing how many animals are moved that way.*
>
> *Once they get here, they are taken care of by our volunteers, it's an all-volunteer organization, no one's paid, so we know why people are here doing what they're doing – because they actually love these animals.*

Maxx's story was one of cruelty. He had a very bad burn on his back, it is healing…He actually had a blowtorch taken to his back, there were others found with him that did not make it, but Maxx did.

There are a lot of fighting rings in the south and in Georgia, and they try to make these dogs mean in order to bait the fighting dog…and the fighting dogs would kill the other dogs of course, but they want them to be competition for them, so they try to make them mean by doing things like this.

When they're leaving, getting into a car with their new owners, they're looking at us like, "Where am I going?" They're starting their life; we all start crying like babies because the moment when I saw their picture on the website, they were dead. No one was going to get them. Then they're going into a home.

Maxx enjoying his new life.

It's fantastic. We can't do it without volunteers. We can't do it without people, good people, who want to give them homes and open up their hearts to them.

Gayle Fitzpatrick, Director
Friends of the Plymouth Pound, Inc.
Plymouth, MA

✦✦✦

Lorraine Ehrhart's group faces social and weather-related challenges in addition to the many other obstacles inhibiting efforts to save Miami's homeless animals.

In South Florida many people don't know what rescue is. When they see us loading twelve to thirteen dogs from one van to another at the Cracker Barrel, they wonder what we're doing. They think we're selling dogs. And when we tell them that we're rescue, usually we get the blank stare and they don't know what you're talking about.

But I think that maybe, hopefully, now it's becoming more politically correct to take in the mutt, to rescue the dog, rather than spend the thousand dollars on the little Teacup Poodle.

The weather has a real impact on the rescue group here and how we work. One thing that people don't realize is that we have an awful lot of thunderstorms here in South Florida, and there are an awful lot of dogs that are petrified from thunderstorms.

Every time that there is bad weather, the influx of dogs being brought to the shelter and lost is enormous, just from thunderstorms. Then we have the threat of the hurricanes.

We had four hurricanes last year where people evacuated and everything. Most shelters, or I think all shelters that will take people in a hurricane, will not take animals, so people are forced to make a decision sometimes.

Prior to a hurricane the line at impound at that county shelter is out the door, people surrendering their animals because bad weather's coming, and they either don't want to take the animal with them or they can't take the animal with them. So the option they choose is to dump the animal at the shelter.

Lorraine Ehrhart, Director
Miami-Dade Rescue Railroad

+++

Janet Northrop can't live with the idea of puppies being destroyed not long after their eyes have opened. Many of the little orphans she cradles in her arms are only a few weeks old, and still long for the warmth of their mothers.

I want to be able to go into the pound and say, "Give me all the ones that you're going to destroy and let me take them and bring them home." I've actually left the pound with as many as twenty-three puppies at one time, and there wasn't a puppy left.

Pound puppies.

I moved into this area and realized there really wasn't a no-kill shelter for stray animals to go. I would call around to try to find out where I could take them and finding out the pounds were pretty much the only place you could take them, and they were going to be destroyed.

Janet gets puppy kisses.

Well I wasn't going to do that, so I just kind of started taking care of them myself, getting them some vet care, finding them homes.

I saw a TV program, it was [about] The Amanda Foundation. I noticed how she would just go into the pounds and say, "I want this one, this one…" She would leave with ten or fifteen dogs, and she actually made her area where no animals had to be euthanized, they had it so under control that no animals were being euthanized.

I just feel like I would like to try to do that for at least the Lincoln County area and hopefully maybe once we get this area good, I would like to help other counties, other pounds. This is basically where I started. I want to start with Lincoln County since I live here.

Janet Northrop, Founder
4 Paws Animal Rescue
Denver, NC

Rande Levine chose to make a career of rescuing after an encounter with an affable Beagle.

Rande Levine and Rufus.

I have vivid memories of walking the shelters, seeing all those sad yet hopeful eyes. I wanted to take them all home. There was one dog in particular that led me down the road to rescue. His name is Rufus, I have had him now fourteen years. He taught me – he showed me – how much joy and balance animal companions add to your life.

I started volunteering for animal rescue organizations. I learned from some of the best the do's and don'ts of animal rescue. I wanted to start my own organization so that more animals would have the opportunity to find homes, as well as give something back to Rufus and his canine friends for teaching me compassion and patience.

Rescue animals have something in their eyes, in their hearts, that is different. They have been abandoned, they know that. Some have been abused, they know that too.

In the overcrowded shelters, sometimes sharing a cage with four other dogs, the life they once knew no longer exists. They go into survival mode, some shut down completely, some become so stressed they get sick. They know; they know that life has changed. When the rescuer comes in to free them of this place, they know they are being saved.

Rande Levine, President
Karma Rescue
Santa Monica, CA

✦✦✦

Erin Burr's on-going adventure with a breed-specific rescue began with a visit to a shelter.

I got started with Maine Coon Rescue after visiting a local shelter here in Maine and leaving with the most beautiful cat I had ever seen. I got on-line to try to identify the breed of cat I brought home and found out he was a beautiful specimen of Maine Coon. No papers of course but he couldn't look more "Coonie".

After sharing our home with him for a few weeks I was in love with everything about him. That led me to do an online search for Maine Coon rescues and that brought me to this wonderful group. The others here were quick to accept my offer to help and the rest is history.

Maine Coon cats are large-boned cats with short hair on their heads and backs getting shaggier on their lower body. They have a lovely, lion-like ruff on their chests, a long fluffy tail, ear furnishings (long hair that protrudes from their ears), lynx tips on the tips of their ears and what is called pantaloons on the backs of their legs.

This helped to protect them from the cold weather of Maine and Canada where these cats are said to originate. They are special due to their intelligence, temperament and their stunning beauty.

Our cats in need of rescue come from many sources. Most come from kill shelters, some from the streets, and some from owners who for many reasons are no longer able to care for their cats. Most go directly into wonderful foster homes to get the much needed TLC that they deserve, and then off to their forever homes.

Our transport volunteers headed up by Carolyn Fitzgerald play an integral part in our ability to help get these cats to safety. Without the folks willing to log endless miles and hours of travel time we would not get these cats moved and therefore would not be able to save countless kitty lives. Kind of like the underground railroad only above ground…

Onnie on cat tree.

Tessa on cat tree.

Like people, all cats react differently. Some handle the ride with nary a peep while others get stressed and react by being quite vocal or even getting what we call a stress-induced upper respiratory infection.

Every cat that I have brought into my home seemed to know that they were spared and acted accordingly. While trust is an issue with any rescued animal they do show gratitude to you in many little cat-like ways. It is hard to put a finger on one thing without sounding silly, but it is something that you just feel and so does the cat.

Erin Burr
Vice President/Eastern Regional Director,
Maine Coon Rescue
Franklin, KY

Stacy LeBaron's group found a solution for feral cats living in colonies along a waterfront area lined with restaurants.

The Merrimack River Feline Rescue Society started in 1992 because we had three hundred cats living on the Newburyport waterfront. There were a lot of restaurants on the waterfront, and when people would have their steak tip dinners out on the decks, the kitties would climb on the patrons' laps and try to have their steak.

In the wintertime, they'd look in the windows, they'd cry and meow while people were having their dinners. So, the cats were becoming a nuisance in Newburyport.

Several residents that had been feeding the cats came to the Chamber of Commerce and said, "We need to do something to help these cats." The head of the Chamber of Commerce at that time owned six cats, so she was truly a lover of cats, and they formed the Merrimack River Feline Rescue Society in 1992.

We have twelve feral cats living on the waterfront right now that are fed out of four feeding stations by thirty-five devoted volunteers who are there twice a day feeding and caring for the kitties. The volunteers are all between twelve to fifteen years of age.

Stacy LeBaron, President
Merrimack River Feline Rescue Society
Salisbury, MA

For homeless cats who are able to live domesticated lives, a natural, home-like environment awaits them at the Society's no-kill sanctuary in Danville, New Hampshire, until they're adopted.

My reason for being involved in this organization is because we are a no-kill organization, and we try and work with every cat and find a place for them, a loving family for them, for all their quirks and jerks that they may have – so we pride ourselves on being able to address the whole cat.

We made a commitment to the cage-less environment here at our sanctuary as well as at our adoption center in Salisbury so that we could really share more of the whole cat with prospective adopters, and it's worked out very well.

We've had some challenges with some of our kitties that hide, but we now have some specially designated volunteers who pay attention to those kitties and try to give them a little extra love and attention and work with socializing them.

Stacy and Ramses.

It's been a huge benefit. People walking in, they'll see three large cat trees and about twelve kitties all sitting around on the cat trees. It's very comfortable, it's a home, it's coming to a cat house — just a lot of happiness and love and joy. There's not sadness.

Stacy LeBaron

Chapter Five
TRANSPORT

After hearing from lots of rescuers, we were eager to interview volunteer drivers. Our plan was to tape the transporters reality-style, while they were actually on the road.

"That's right," I explained to the drivers over the phone. "We'll have one camera operator in the transport vehicle while another rides along in the equipment truck to tape the hand-off as it happens."

"Along with interviewing drivers en route," I continued, "we'd like to get close-ups of the dogs and cats on board, to try to see things from the animals' point of view."

Like almost everything I've ever wanted to share with the viewing public, this was easier said than done. How were we supposed to tape a transport when everyone we contacted seemed terrified of being on camera? Were there no wanna-be actors and actresses hidden amongst the transporter troops?

Although a few brave souls came forward and said we could stick cameras in their faces while they were driving, they weren't in succession on the transport schedule. The problems arose when Sara said, "Sure, you can tape me on my way to Portsmouth," but Bob, who would be receiving the animal from Sara replied, "No way, I'm not gonna be on any TV show."

A few times when we got permissions squared away with everyone involved and had our crew all ready to go, the transports were cancelled. All we had in the can after months of hard work was a bunch of good interviews. So far, the documentary amounted to little more than a lullaby. It was talking heads only, and I knew there would be no audience for that. Discouraged, I wondered how we would ever get this show on the road.

A few days later our luck changed and I announced to Russ, my soul mate and production partner, that we had a special assignment coming up. We would soon be transporting a little brown-eyed girl, a passenger covered with fur! I wasn't really sure what to expect on our first transport, so I took some time to review my notes. Sandy had talked about what can happen once rescued animals are on the road.

> *As far as the actual transport, a little bit of everything can happen. They can run very far behind schedule… we've had dogs who have gotten away during transports…There have been some dogs who have gotten lost at roadside parks, so you really want to know you're working with people who know what they're doing, know about certain types of collars they're not gonna slip out of, and are prepared to deal with some dogs that may be terrified.*
>
> *Sandy Clabaugh*
> *Almost Home Dachshund Rescue*

Since we didn't fall into the category of "people who know what they're doing," I thought I had better chat with some drivers before our first transport had a chance to become our last. Most of the drivers I conversed with had become utterly hooked somewhere along that very first journey with a rescued animal.

After exchanging emails with Frank and Ted in New Jersey, "Teddy" informed me that the transport vehicle they drove was an old truck covered with rescue magnets, and that I probably shouldn't keep referring to them as "gentlemen."

> *Don't be offended but the Ted in "frankandted" is a girl, me. Ted is short for Theodora. Frank is my husband of almost a year now. We were married on a Saturday morning in April and drove a transport run that afternoon.*

Where do I start? With the babes on the trip? No, it all starts with Hershey, our first adoptee who came to us through friends. An angel wrapped in fur, but we still had no idea of the plight of these poor souls nationwide. Then about eight months later I decided he needed a companion, a sister to keep him company when we had to be away, and so the hunt began.

After numerous disappointments on Petfinder.com, there she was, my baby looking back at me from the computer screen with the caption "Last One." Last of a litter of eight little girls only seven weeks old, she had been dumped at a pound and rescued by a two-legged saviour.

After a flurry of emails and Mapquest printings we loaded up the truck and off the three of us went on the 884-mile seventeen-hour round-trip to bring home our baby.

I knew nothing of rescue and kill shelters and transport but I was about to learn. Through some quirk of fate, I met through the internet a wonderful warm-hearted soul in Texas and with a keyboard we became good friends. I had the motivation to pursue this rescue thing but she (although she may not know it) provided the drive.

To condense, my other half and I have signed on with two groups dedicated to moving these angels, who through no fault of their own find themselves in dire need of being transported from certain death to safety and a bright new future.

After what seemed like a lifetime, lo and behold along comes one close enough for us to help. Off went the email offering, and back came the answer, "Okay, you're in." My heart was pounding so hard I could hardly breath as I raced out of my office to tell Frank.

"It's us, we're going!!" I spent a week emailing back and forth and praying it wouldn't get cancelled. Checking with other drivers and looking for updates. Relaying message after message. The final post comes, everything is set, all legs are filled, we are good to go.

Dawn of the morning, my two furkids are restless and want to go out at 5:00 am. Oh man, I need to be rested and alert today of all days – but they are my babies and so I hold them off 'til 6:00 am and do what all good mommies are expected to do and give in to their wants and needs.

Okay, now it's time to go. We are leaving ours behind today and sad eyes look at us as I explain to them why Mommy and Daddy have to go, and they understand. Off we go with a borrowed cell phone, mountains of directions, other cell phone numbers (the lifeline that ties us together), two little rawhide shoes I got for the babes, bottles of water, a bowl, puppy biscuits and poop bags.

On the road yakking about dog this and dog that – when did my life become all about dogs??? Is there life without dogs??? – we get to Delaware and proceed to get lost. Okay, regroup, read map and head for the meeting place. On the way comes a call from the leg coming to meet us, they are mired in traffic and running behind.

That's okay, I laughingly admit to them. We are lost anyway. No sweat, we'll head to the meeting place and wait for them. Frank can take a nap.

Okay, we're there, and the next thing you know a silver Taurus pulls up next to us and two women come over and say, "You're here for the pups, right?

Of course they knew us. Our info and description of the fifteen-year-old Bronco we have is on the final post sent to each driver. "Yeah that's us, glad to meet ya."

Short time goes by and here comes the blue Windstar we are anxiously waiting for and as it rolls by a window goes down and shouts of "Are you here for the dogs??" All hands fly up in the air waving with shouts back of, "Yeah it's us!"

Seconds later we are handed two of the sweetest angels I have ever seen. I scoop up one and she licks my face and nuzzles my neck with the absolute trust only an innocent can have.

I hand her off to Frank and pick up the little boy. He is quiet and calm and smaller and thinner than his sister. There are pictures and handshakes and, "Glad to meet ya, hope to see you again soon, really looking forward to the next run" type things and off we go.

Babes in the back of the Bronco walking around and chewing on the rawhide shoes. Little girl comes to the front seat and whimpers and not too many minutes later the whimpers become a full-blown howl.

Okay, I give in and both are lifted to the sanctuary of the front seats with Frank and me and my lap. Little boy curls up on my lap and sleeps the rest of the trip. Little girl wiggles around a bit then scoots off to the floor and stretches out and nods off.

While driving along, my hand caressing the little bundle snoozing peacefully on, I say to my copilot, "Can you believe they were going to kill these babes, wonderful innocent angels each with their own distinct personality already?"

Of course we got lost again, but finally managed to find the hand-off spot. Pile out of the truck, babes on leash. Our little man takes one look at the woman walking toward us and begins to bark furiously, this from the one who had not made a peep the entire trip. I choose to believe he was protecting us from what he perceived to be a stranger, a quality endearing to all dogs large and small, old and young.

I cannot begin to find the words to describe the feelings I had, the joy at being a part of their lives if only for a brief time, the overwhelming sense of well-being in knowing that I – no we, he and I are in this together, a team – had a hands-on part in saving two precious lives.

These babes looked at us with such unconditional trust. I had them for only minutes and they were kissing my face and curling up in my lap to drift off into uninhibited sleep while I held their little paws with one hand and whispered to them how beautiful they are, keeping the other hand curled around fragile frames.

There are no words to give you the feeling of holding their warm little bodies and knowing that you had some part in their escape. They truly are miraculous creatures and every time one is **needlessly** lost it is an irrevocable sin against humankind.

Man, I can't wait to do it again, to touch the lives of angels no matter how fleeting, who would not have survived if not for caring, devoted people who selflessly give of themselves, people like us. How about that: we're part of the group now.

There are two tiny little holes in my heart where the two we handed over briefly lived, and the truck never seemed so empty as it did on the ride home. But nine hours after our departure we arrived home to a furious flurry of tails, tongues and paws.

I explained to them that Mommy and Daddy had been with angels – had held them, kissed their noses, patted their heads one last time and sent them on their way. And that we had missed them and were glad to be home and, for the moment, all was right in the world.

As a postscript, we found out shortly after getting home that "our" little girl has already been adopted…man are they in for a ride, she is a PIP.

We learned of our first transport through TruckNPaws and shortly after joined the rescue group we drove for, FOR Animals Inc., which is based in Rocky Mount, North Carolina with a branch in our home state of New Jersey. Since then we have fostered for them, helped with adoptions, and continue to transport almost every Saturday.

I have also recently joined a wonderful group, SPIN – SavingPyrsInNeed, based in Texas as a long-distance member, and have helped them with a home visit here on *the East Coast among other things. The internet rescue network is amazing.*

Theodora (Teddy) Wambold
Volunteer Animal Transporter

Donna Alexander's first assignment as a volunteer driver required that she transport the tiniest of passengers.

I was never a big animal lover until I got married and my husband wanted a dog. We got Kramer the Pomeranian and it was all over for me. I fell in love.

About a year later we adopted Cosmo, the Sheltie mix, from a local shelter. I started doing some research and ran across an article about the puppy mills and my heart was breaking for these animals. I never knew such places existed and I wanted to help.

Besides monetary donations I found out about Truck-NPaws, a transport group for Puppy Mill Rescue. I signed up on their transport list and soon afterwards I was part of other rescue lists.

It's a very tight-knit community. I run into the same people all the time on these transports. I did a transport for a lady in Minnesota that knows a lady that runs a Chow Chow rescue in Ohio that my in-laws adopted two Chows from.

My mother-in-law did a site check in Illinois for the lady in Minnesota. We did not find out that we all knew each other until after my transport. It's a small world. I also do home visits for many rescue groups that require them in the Chicagoland area.

I would like to share a story with you about one of my transports. It was my very first one and encompassed about seventy-five miles one way. My mother-in-law decided to come with me since both of us are dog lovers and she wanted to see what this was all about.

We set off to Rockford, Illinois, to pick up a tiny Pekingese that was originally a puppy mill dog, but now has found a forever home. It was a two-day transport to get him to his new Mommy, after which she was to drive another three hundred miles or so to get him home.

When we picked little Gizmo up from our contact at the Cracker Barrel, he was sitting in back of her car shaking. He was this tiny little ball of fur. I sat down with him in the back seat of the previous driver's car and started to talk to him.

He seemed to be warming up to me so I picked him up and took him into our car. My mother-in-law was driving while I had Gizmo on my lap. He was settling in for the ride but keeping a watchful eye on us.

After about fifteen minutes Gizmo felt at ease and started to snore. He curled up on my lap not to be heard from for the rest of the trip (well, except for his loud snoring).

I fell so in love with this little pupper that had he not been going to his forever home, I would have filled out an adoption application immediately. It was hard to imagine that this sweet adorable boy was living in a puppy mill, never touching grass or having any human contact.

It was a great ending. I even kept in touch with his new Mom for a while. My next transport was a 150-pound mixed breed dog that was the sweetest guy in the world.

He greeted you by standing on his hind legs and giving you a big old kiss with his big old tongue. Other transports included cats and puppies. Each one has its own story and it's a great feeling knowing that you can play just a tiny little part in saving these wonderful animals.

My husband always worries that we will end up with ten dogs and cats because after every transport I fall in love with the animals and want to take them home. The *people who organize this are awesome. What we do is the easy part.*

Donna S. Alexander
Illinois

While sifting through stories from drivers, I learned that not all rescued animals travel on the ground. Pilots with small planes aid these animals in getting to their destinations when there's a great distance to cover and a ground transport just isn't feasible.

Kevin Boyle is one such volunteer pilot. He agreed to fly in from New Jersey to meet us at a small airport on the north shore of Massachusetts.

Kevin taxied slowly down the runway abutting the Great Salt Marsh at Plum Island Airfield. He was in his prized Cessna Skyhawk and it was a brilliantly sunny, blistering hot June day.

I was especially glad to meet him because we had tried on five other occasions to get together. It was either too snowy, too rainy, too cloudy, or too windy on the other days. Weather conditions have to be just right for small planes to fly, Kevin told me, or – well, we all know what can happen.

When Kevin stepped out of the plane and shook hands with our small three-person crew, I liked him immediately. I remember peering into the plane's claustrophobic passenger seat thinking, "There's no way you'll get ME up in the air."

What I really wanted to know was how he used his small craft to help animals.

> *I got involved in flying rescued animals several years ago when I adopted a dog from a local rescue group, and I learned about the problem with homeless animals. So I began helping with the rescue groups and the animal shelters and then somebody learned that I was a private pilot and asked me to fly dogs from West Virginia to New Jersey, and it's what I've been doing ever since then.*

I'm normally known as the last-minute person — if somebody calls me up on a Friday night and we know the weather's gonna be good on Saturday, that's usually the best situation for us to do the air transports.

Kevin Boyle
Volunteer Pilot

I imagined a sky-loving Boston Terrier sitting next to Kevin in the plane with paws on the window, taking in the view. That's not how it works in Kevin's manual of procedures for flying rescued animals…

The animal's safety is very important when I transport them, they're all transported in dog crates and cat kennels and they're confined within the airplane, and that's how we keep them safe.

We only transport animals in approved pet carriers… and all the animals need to be checked by a vet to go on the plane. They need to have a health certificate: normally we're taking them across state lines, and that's a requirement.

Kevin walked around the plane and demonstrated the safety check he does before a flight. He checked the fins by moving them back and forth, then seemed to be looking for leaks. I felt the sun's rays cook me from the inside out, and all of us turned red. We talked about where the needy animals come from.

Volunteer animal transport is so important because there are so many dogs in rural places that just don't stand a chance to be adopted unless there are people that can transport them to bigger cities.

I transport dogs of all different sizes. The Golden Retrievers are very popular so when we do find them in the rural shelters, we transport them back because they can be adopted easily in the major cities. My role is to get them from these rural places to places where they're more likely to be adopted.

Okay Kevin, since I'm terrified of leaving the ground, I wonder if animals are afraid to fly?

> *Actually, I think the animals kind of enjoy it. They have a nice comfortable seat in the back in a safe and secure transport crate, and I think when the engine starts up it lulls them to sleep, and I've never had a problem. They've always been peaceful, quiet flights.*

What about the logistics of a rescue flight? How are they put together?

> *They all start when somebody contacts us with a need to transport some animals. I'll research where the people are on the receiving end and on the destination, and we'll find out where there's a small airport nearby (there's about ten thousand small airports throughout the country), and then we'll plan a flight, schedule a time and, as long as their weather is good, we'll fly to the airport.*

Kevin Boyle, a transporter with wings!

> *Somebody will bring the animals to that airport, we'll load them up in the airplane, and bring them back to the destination where there will be rescue people waiting to pick them up and take them to their foster or permanent home.*

And what types of animals are you asked to fly?

> *My rescuing of animals is not limited to cats and dogs. I'll fly just about any type of domestic animal that will fit on the airplane...Not too long ago I was contacted and asked if I could transport a pig from Lancaster,*

*Pennsylvania, to Albany, New York. My first reaction was
that the pig was going to be too big and too heavy for the
plane, but they assured me that she was a little miniature
potbelly, and she weighed about fifty pounds.*

So we set everything up, we picked her up and we

*transferred her up there and every-
thing went fine. I guess you could
say that pigs flew that day.*

When pigs fly!

I was getting excited. I noticed there
were lots of retired pilots just hanging
out at this quaint, family-friendly little
airport. Some of them had already told
me about their canine flight buddies
while we were having lunch. Could any of these guys be candidates
for animal rescue in the skies? Perhaps with a little nudging from
Kevin...

*I would absolutely encourage other pilots to get in-
volved with this, especially those who love animals. I would
advise them to check with their local rescue groups, check
with the internet, see which groups need help transporting,
and volunteer!*

There also seemed to be a number of would-be pilots on the airfield and at the buffet table, too. Maybe Kevin could recruit a few.

*If somebody would like to get involved, the first thing
they need to do is get their private pilot's license. They can
go on the internet, find out the requirements for that. It's
relatively simple. It takes about forty hours of training, and
then they're ready to go.*

I thought about Kevin's generosity as he re-fueled his plane.
Fuel prices keep climbing, and yet he keeps flying animals deemed
desperate and out of time. What's the payoff for doing this, Kevin?

*I really enjoy doing this because it gives me a chance
to combine two things that I love – animals and flying air-
planes. I get the satisfaction of knowing that some very nice*

dogs and cats are going to find homes by bringing them to the rescue groups that arrange these transports.

Kevin left as a group of clouds rolled in and clumped themselves in the air spaces he needed to fly through. I could tell he wasn't fond of clouds, and really paid attention to the weather, as all good pilots do.

As the Skyhawk cleared the runway and eventually disappeared, I thought about the flying potbellied pig, and wondered where she had ended up. My curiosity led me to Joyce at Forgotten Friends Rescue, who was happy to fill me in.

As for Maggie, she is still with us. I found out about Maggie because she was being given up by her owner. She came to us from another pig rescuer who I had emailed on a pig rescue list. I always wanted to have the experience of housing a housebroken pig.

We have come to love and adore her. I asked Kevin to fly her because I felt it would be less stressful for her as when I had to do a transport of another larger potbellied pig on the ground – it was very stressful for her and us.

The van that moved her had the air conditioning go down on a very, hot humid day and we had to stop every few miles to wet her down with bottles and bottles of cold water. It was nice though, because many places where we stopped people came over to help wet her down, buy her cold iced teas, and give donations when they found out what we were doing.

We currently house eleven donkeys, four horses, four pigs, thirteen dogs, seven cats and a few domestic birds.

I was always a "rescuer." I brought home strays from the time I was a little kid. My grandfather taught me to love and respect animals. He had always told me that God put everything on this earth to serve a purpose and we were not here to destroy it just because we could. My father (his son) was very abusive to us and I found in animals a

sincerity and love that was and has always been uncondi-
tional. There is such a feeling when you see an animal who
was neglected and or abused accept you and show you they
know you care for them.

Joyce Urban
Forgotten Friends Pet Rescue
Sharon Springs, NY

✦✦✦

Russ and I were notified by email that Blondie, the mixed-breed puppy we would be transporting would soon be on her way. Blondie had a screened and approved adoptive family in Maine who couldn't wait to lay their eyes on her.

The family, a young military couple who lived just outside the base, would drive south, pick her up somewhere in Massachusetts and take her home. We were scheduled to drive the last leg before handing Blondie off to her forever family.

A Georgia-based coordinator for a transport already underway offered to take little Blondie along. She was listed on the run sheet posted by Donna Carpenter as a hitchhiker, and somehow she was labeled as a yellow-Lab mix.

Passengers for this transport included a black and white male Cocker Spaniel named Rosco, and Ernie, a Cocker/Terrier mix. Rosco and Ernie were traveling from Georgia to Maryland. Janet Northrop would meet the transport as it went through North Carolina, where she would hand the pup off to the driver.

Many coordinators choose to name their transports, particularly if they have more than one transport scheduled over the same weekend. Blondie's transport was aptly dubbed "Snowy Run," and it was late on a cold Saturday in January that weather wreaked havoc on a perfectly executed plan.

Rosco and Ernie's first driver, Dixie, left Georgia at 6 am. She and the dogs were in Gastonia, North Carolina, by ten o'clock to meet Bettina, who was also waiting for Blondie. The seven-week-old hitchhiker rode with four different volunteer drivers before she arrived in Durham, North Carolina, which put a lot of stress on such a little girl.

The heavy snow and treacherous roads combined with poor visibility meant the dogs could not go on to Alexandria, Virginia; and Amanda, who was scheduled to drive the Baltimore leg backed out. It was becoming too dangerous to be on the road. The three dogs stayed overnight with Helen in Durham because the transporter en route to meet her had to turn around and go home. It was still too slippery and unsafe to drive the next morning, so Snowy Run was postponed until Monday.

Melisa met Helen on Monday morning and took the three dogs to Alexandria, where they met Ernie's adopter. Ernie's adoption was finalized on the spot and he went home.

A volunteer from a local rescue group named Chris picked up Rosco and left for Baltimore to meet Amanda. The driver who had backed out of the transport due to bad weather had jumped back in to help. Meanwhile, Blondie was driven to Frederick, Maryland, by yet another volunteer – Lisa.

Chris and Amanda met at the Hilton Hotel parking lot, and Amanda took Rosco to Delaware to meet up with his adopter. Blondie made it safely to a temporary foster home with Linda, where she would stay and rest for a while before she would hitch yet another ride north on a transport leaving Hagerstown. It was the next day, Tuesday, that Blondie's troubles began.

Linda, an experienced rescuer and foster Mom, reported that Blondie had vomited, and that she wouldn't eat. She decided to try giving Blondie goat's milk, something she had used successfully with sick pups in the past. By Wednesday, Blondie looked listless and didn't want to play. That evening, she worsened.

Reading the flurry of emails speedily sent back and forth between myself, Linda, Janet, and her adoptive Mom, I began to fear the worst. I was afraid "my" little pup, our very first transport, was dying. Linda scheduled a vet visit for early the following morning, where Blondie was diagnosed with coccidia.

My vet was very worried and perplexed until we got the fecal results as the lack of diarrhea threw us off about the cause. She got fluid (which was leaking out – and we discovered a flea biting her right where the fluid was leaking)…her temp is sub-normal so I have her in a very warm room (where I keep my canary) in her crate right by the baseboard heat – Dr. Dodson said I'd not overheat her there.

As long as her temp comes up and she rallies it should still be OK this weekend…just don't want her to go until her body temp is stabilized (it's just too cold to take chances) but there is a good chance she could bounce back quickly… she is on a 10-day course of Albon so if she goes the adopter will HAVE to complete that. We just need to be able to reach the transport sometime Saturday if we decide it's a "no" – otherwise I'd say just figure on her being there.

Thanks for all of you being there for Blondie and me… I'd have taken her to the vet anyway but I do appreciate that you all offered support without judgment. I have been heartsick over her – it's good to have an answer.

Linda

When I looked up coccidia in a medical library, I found that the infection is especially widespread in young animals housed in groups (shelters, rescue areas, kennels, etc.,) and that it's a common parasite. Blondie's transport coordinator was glad to hear that the diagnosis was one of a treatable condition rather than something like parvo, a contagious killer of young dogs.

Janet was bothered by what the smallest pup of the litter had endured. Convinced that stress was most likely a factor in all of this, she decided that from now on, her pups would need to be at least three months of age to ride on a transport.

Jessa, Blondie's adoptive Mom, wished she could have been there to comfort her new puppy during her ordeal. I was beginning to wonder if I would ever get the chance to hold little Blondie in my arms.

♦♦♦

I had been trying to find out where this whole animal transport system originated, but no one seemed to know. When I posed the question to Brandy Holleran, one of the list owners, she graciously shared her experiences in the transport arena, and explained how her service grew to assist animals nationwide.

A Truck Driver With an Idea

After acquiring my first Papillon as a gift from my hubby, I joined several Papillon groups, and discovered rescue there. As a truck driver, I knew there was a way I could help with the transportation of rescued animals – aka "the furkids." So I simply got some help to set up a website, and began posting my truck routes.

Not being familiar with websites, I left the site "open" and much to my surprise, people began joining! Soon I had requests for transports all over the nation. I began reaching out to friends and family and some of my Papillon rescue group people to help move these furkids. And in the meantime, more people joined.

On the Road Again (OTRA) was designed to combine the assistance of over-the-road truck drivers with that of private vehicle individuals to more quickly and efficiently expedite the transport of our furkids. OTRA has grown to over 2,500 transport contact members in just a little over one year.

We are working to make OTRA sort of a one-stop-shopping place where people with rescue needs can come and find a rescue for an animal, a coordinator for a transport, and then the coordinator can find drivers to fill the "legs" of that transport.

Some of the finest rescue people are from other countries. One of our verified members is a coordinator from Canada. She draws from our group as well as some Canadian ones to fill her transports.

A List Owner's To-Do List

Being a list owner is very time-consuming, especially as the list grows. Approximately five to nine thousand emails cross our boards daily.

A list owner must read most of them.

A list owner must also keep petty squabbles from breaking out on the board, defuse any potential arguments, and sometimes even settle disputes. The list owner and his/her moderators must verify that the receiving rescues are valid, and that the transporters are qualified to transport.

We must make sure the animal is vetted, altered and current on vaccinations, and also make sure that shelter animals without a waiting period in a temporary foster home never travel with vetted non-shelter animals, so as to minimize the possible spread of any infectious disease.

Before Technology

I transported before the technology was in place, but not to any great extent. Contact information was a closely guarded thing then, and few coordinators shared with each other. Now many of us share with all in order to better assist more animals.

In the beginning, it was one person who wanted to help who called a neighbor or relative in another town further up the trek, that made the underground rescue work. I suspect it probably began simultaneously in several places with different individuals, but needed the technology to grow by leaps and bounds as it has done in recent years.

I know coordinators who have done the exact same thing. They are still coordinating, but now use the technology available to better assist the furbabies.

Brandy Holleran
OTRA Founder/List Owner

Joyce Urban remembers what it was like before coordinators could meet up with drivers in cyberspace.

> *Ground transports for the animals started many years ago using the phone lines to contact other people — it was very hard. You had to know someone who knew someone who maybe could help. But little by little transport coordinators grew out of these calls.*
>
> *I have a friend who used to be the "queen of transports" and rescues because she maintained a binder with alphabetical lists of names and addresses and phone numbers of people willing to help. She could also cross-reference it for the breed of animals the rescuers would take in. Sadly a serious injury ended her reign.*
>
> *Joyce Urban*
> *Forgotten Friends Pet Rescue*

OTRA Moderators and Members

> *We moderate our group. I have been lucky enough to locate several individuals who moderate various areas in the nation. Anything that crosses the board beginning in their respective areas is theirs to check into and if valid, try to help fill. Of course, all moderators are OTRA verified.*
>
> *If an individual wishes to join our group, they may easily do so as it is open joining. However, before they can transport or rescue with us, we require at least two valid rescue references with whom they have worked in the past, and validation of their vetting practices from their veterinarian.*
>
> *We check these references carefully, and in the process we explain the reason for our group. Usually, the individuals listed as references for the first person join as well, and are subsequently also verified. In this way we also acquire a listing for veterinarians in many areas, just in case of an emergency during transport.*

At times, transport and rescue can be exasperating. So many animals and too few transporters! Also, truckers must adhere to a strict time schedule so as to be able to make their delivery and pick-up appointments. Many of our people have met for the hand-off at ungodly hours in the AM so that the furkid could catch its ride to safety.

Friends and Family

My friends have complained a bit that rescue takes up too much of my time (it does!), but I have found that my good friends will support me in this endeavor, and some will actually help as well. I have made so many new friends in rescue and transport that I do not miss those that could not understand my desire to save the animals.

I would not be able to do what I do without the support of my wonderful hubby and family! My husband and brother both drive trucks and carry the furbabies for OTRA.

Larry (my hubby) doesn't complain overmuch when he comes home to find three or four new furkids here that I am fostering, or providing a temporary "hold" for, or just "overnighting" to allow them to begin their journey the following day anew.

Attitude/Behavior Challenges

There are always culture-specific challenges to be faced in any area. I am from Kentucky, where hunters meet for large raccoon and other hunts, hunt their dogs, and simply drop off at the shelter those animals which did not perform adequately, knowing perfectly well all the while that the furkids are nearly always doomed when they are disposed of thusly.

Other hunters simply knock the animals in the head or shoot them rather than take the time to drive to the desper-

ately inadequate shelters. This also happens in Tennessee quite frequently.

Georgia regulations are in place fairly well, and other than the local farmer losing his animal – and rather than looking for it, just acquiring another – we do fairly well here, although the attitude of many people is that the animals are "disposable pets."

On the other hand, some of the most dedicated rescue people I know are located in these three states, so it is not just here: this attitude sadly seems to prevail throughout much of the nation. But again, on the up-side, more and more people are becoming aware of animal rescue, and are also becoming more responsive to the needs of their furry four-legged partners in life.

Geese On Board...

We transport any of God's creatures. Our transporters have helped to carry dogs, kitties, guinea pigs, bunnies, chickens, white mice, peacocks, birds (parrots and canaries), a couple of horses (including a miniature one), spiders, snakes, pot-bellied pigs, a three-legged duck, and a flock of geese, to name a few.

Bird transport requires some specific knowledge because if they are panicked, the creatures will possibly harm themselves in their fright. Same with horses and, of course, special equipment is needed for the transport.

Special knowledge is also required for other animals, and all transporters must be aware of the general guidelines for transporters: never allow the animal off lead, retain a firm grasp on the lead at all times, how often to walk and feed, water, to check for any signs of illness, etc.

Too Many Groups?

There can never be too many (or even "enough") rescues and transport groups. To believe that, one only needs to gather the statistics on how many animals are euthanized each day.

The Emotional Toll

Dealing with urgent life and death posts and requests for help on a daily basis is spiritually and emotionally draining. I cry a lot.

Yes, it is true that sometimes we lose one that has touched us deeply, and then the tears flow. During these times, we in rescue reach out to each other for support and we receive it, because those we reach out to have either been there themselves, or know they will be at some point in the future.

In Times of Disaster

I helped transport a few of the hurricane-rescued animals, although I did not coordinate or moderate any of the transports. I was more involved with gathering and forwarding supplies to our OTRA Alabama moderator, which she in turn carried into the relief area.

OTRA was instrumental in moving several loads of animal food, crates and cages, bedding, medical supplies, etc., in for the animals, as well as food, water, diapers and clothing for the human victims.

The supplies were gathered from as far away as New Jersey and Pennsylvania, and donations for fuel for the OTRA bus, which carried the supplies, came in from nearly every corner of the nation. The bus itself was loaned to OTRA by a rescue person…

Those animals that I did help transport were either very frightened by their experience and so were very timid, or were overjoyed to have human companionship once again, and so were very friendly.

OTRA'S Darling

Tarot is a little blind senior miniature Chow. She is now and will forever be our OTRA mascot/flag doggie. Tarot, considered "disposable" because of her age and failing sight, was unceremoniously dumped by her owner at the time in her life when she needed her human most.

Fortunately, she was rescued by Judy H. with Seven Bells Sanctuary, and a search began for the perfect forever home for this tiny little girl. One was located in Florida with Sue G., who takes in "special needs" animals and trains blind furkids to the sound of bells...the perfect home for a very precious and deserving doggie.

But poor little Tarot was nowhere near Florida! Judy was based in Missouri, and so the underground rescue railroad swung into action. Judy located a terrific transport coordinator in Deanna F. in Minnesota through her Chow rescue. Deanna designed a run sheet (the transporter's Bible), and began posting the transport.

It crossed the OTRA board, of course, and I saw it. Knowing my hubby's trucking route would take him through the area, I contacted Deanna to advise that he could carry this little girl most of the way to her forever home, and that is exactly what happened!

I had the pleasure of overnighting Tarot, and a sweeter little doggie cannot be found. When Larry handed her off to her forever mommy in Florida, Sue snapped a photo while wiping the tears of joy from her eyes.

Larry Holleran and Tarot.

Now we all refer to Tarot as "our" Tarot, and Sue is kind enough to send us updates and pictures of herself *holding her as they rock together in the big old rocking chair that Tarot has come to love so much.*

It is stories like these that make rescue so worth all the grief and anxiety over the lost ones we cannot save.

Brandy Holleran

♦♦♦

The general consensus between all parties involved was that Blondie should stay with Linda and recuperate for two weeks before going home. It was also decided that a volunteer driver-to-driver transport from Maryland to Maine would be too stressful, and could cause Blondie to relapse back into declining health.

I checked in with Linda a week later for an update on Blondie's condition.

> Oh my – what a handful now that she's feeling good!!!
>
> She's gaining weight nicely and her belly is getting fat – and out pops a little umbilical hernia, nothing to be concerned about at her age, many pups have them.
>
> The adopter will need to be very careful – she loves to drag a leash around and if none is available she looks for electric cords. I'm trying to get her to stay away from them but have to watch her, like the baby she is: she is into everything.
>
> Linda

An alternative to the driver-to-driver transport was found. For fifty dollars, Blondie could ride north on a horse trailer specially outfitted for dogs all the way to New England. The business owner and driver was a former rescuer who had a relationship with thirty different rescue groups who adopted dogs to New England. He stated that his mission was simply to provide a low-cost means to transport dogs, and to provide a healthy environment for them throughout their trip. His travel requirements were strict – every dog had to be up to date on vaccinations including rabies, spayed or neutered, and accompanied by a recent Certificate of Health.

His other firm stipulation was that each animal had to have been away from a shelter for a minimum of two weeks before boarding the transport. There were health risks with dogs coming directly from shelters he explained, and it was to everyone's benefit to have the dogs spend time at a vet's office, a kennel, or a foster home before joining up with other travelers on the trailer.

When I asked the driver about his impetus for creating the transport service he said that, like any entrepreneur, he saw a need in the animal transport world and provided the means to fill it. As a rescuer, he had often witnessed transports falling apart and being cancelled because of one or two missing legs. Rather than let the draining task of coordinating be for naught, a rescue group could now choose to hire him to plug the gap in a transport and potentially save an out-of-time dog.

This man was obviously all about the dogs, and in addition to providing a climate-controlled ride he had an assistant along to make sure the dogs were walked, fed, and checked on at regular intervals. Aware of Blondie's size and frail condition, the driver offered to keep her crate in his back seat, where she could be very closely monitored.

Linda met the paid transport at 1:00 a.m. on a Saturday in mid-February and handed her foster pup off to the driver. She never complained about meeting the transport at such an inconvenient hour.

She had expected to have Blondie as an overnight guest, but ended up caring for her for more than two weeks. During that time, Linda loved her, consoled her, patiently fed her with a large medicine dropper, administered her medication, played with her, took her to two vet appointments, and did lots of other things that a recovering pup requires.

Linda sent me a note the night before she sent Blondie on her way:

> It's been wonderful working with you and I know
> - in view of all that has happened - that the
> rescue that took her in has to be a good one.
>
> If I can ever help in getting dogs up to your
> area just let me know. Paul and I enjoy road
> trips and often do very long transport legs.
> We went from Frederick to Allentown PA and then
> to Takoma Park MD (just across the line from
> Washington DC) this past Saturday to pick up
> and deliver a collie.
>
> It was an all day trip (and Blondie had to
> have a puppy-sitter - thank God for teen-aged
> grandchildren) but it was well worth it to get
> this dog home.
>
> Looking forward to getting to meet you
> someday also ... we do come up to NY from time
> to time so maybe we can come a bit farther ;-)
> it might be a nice way to escape the oppressive
> heat in this area sometime this summer.
>
> Linda Kleiner
> MerryLea Rescue
> Frederick, MD

On Sunday afternoon, Russ and I received the long awaited call from the driver transporting Blondie. He was running on schedule and would meet us at the appointed time. We left nervously excited, hoping we hadn't forgotten anything.

Driving in to our pre-arranged meeting place an hour later, we could see smiling faces everywhere. People with leashes, children, crates, bags. Each person who walked to the open side of the horse trailer came away squealing with delight, and hugging a dog!

We walked around the corner and I said to the driver, with anxious anticipation, "I'm here for little Blondie, please." He politely asked for my ID as we had only spoken over the telephone. As he inspected it, I looked inside the trailer.

It was warm, clean, and very organized. A few big dogs were left waiting to be let out of their crates. The driver, who had stepped up to the back seat, picked up a crate that looked like it had nothing in it with a bag attached to the side.

When I saw her, all six pounds of her, I covered my mouth with my hand. I didn't want the driver to hear me gasp at the sight of the most beautiful puppy I had ever seen.

She was wearing a red sweater and a sparkly collar and for a moment, she didn't even look real. When she wiggled to the front of the carrier, it was as if an enchanting doll was coming to life. Her yellow-goldish fur glistened against the red yarn in the sweater, and her eyes were huge and dark brown.

Russ couldn't believe what she looked like either. We had never seen a puppy like this before, and so while he set her crate securely in the back seat of our truck, I thanked the driver for his watchfulness over this canine baby and bade him farewell.

Though I wanted her to ride in my lap for our hour together, Russ was against it. He was afraid she might fall, or get car sick, or jump on him while he was trying to drive. He wanted Blondie to arrive safely and so I just gazed at her, and let her teethe happily on my fingers for most of the ride.

Peering into her bag, I found all kinds of items Linda had lovingly packed. Toys, a play rope, special food, vet records, bottled water to aid her transition to Maine's water, lots of instructions for the adoptive family, contacts numbers, everything a puppy would need to start a new life....

When we drove in to the restaurant parking lot, I was thrilled to see that the adopters hadn't arrived. Now was my chance, I would open the carrier door and hold little Blondie on my lap.

She came to me willingly, but with a measure of uncertainty that seemed to say, "Please don't hurt me. I'm scared and very vulnerable, and I've been with lots and lots of strangers since I was taken from my mother, my sisters, and my brothers."

I put her in my lap and kissed her gently on the head, expecting to bump into her halo. A feeling of sheer joy engulfed me, and then the unexpected happened.

Blondie looked up at me slowly, deliberately, tenderly. She fixed her voluminous eyes on mine, and there it was. The look! The look the rescuer had talked about! The look that said, "I could have died if not for you." Her eyes pierced me with what I recognized to be this little one's relief, hopefulness and gratitude.

I turned to Russ and before I could silently mouth, "Get the camera!" he said, disappointedly, "We forgot it." In our haste to arrive on time for Blondie, we had grabbed our digital camera but had left the broadcast camera behind.

A few seconds later, a young woman with long blonde hair walked over to the truck with her husband, a big and handsome guy. The neatly dressed couple had a sleeping baby with them and when I handed Blondie to Jessa, it appeared she couldn't speak.

She hadn't expected Blondie to be so small or so beautiful and was happy as could be. My sadness at letting the pup go after our all-too-short time together was assuaged by her new family's bliss.

Jessa's husband made sure all of Blondie's belongings were handed over to him and her crate was fastened next to the baby's car seat. They would grow up together, Blondie and this little baby boy.

I almost felt guilty over my thoughts as they drove away. I hoped Jessa would have time in her day to properly care for two babies (one human and one not), and I'll admit I hoped that Blondie would know to move quickly if the baby teetered over in her path when he became a toddler.

Russ and I felt empty all the way home. The back seat where Blondie had been was bare and lonely. It had all been so brief, and poof! Our sixty or so minutes with her had expired, and she was carried away.

I wasn't aware of it then, but we were experiencing many of the same feelings shared by other volunteer transporters, and especially first-timers. We had gone through an emotional roller coaster of an initiation, and now we were in the club.

"Well," I remarked to Russ, "maybe now that we've actually transported a puppy, it will be easier to hook up with a transport coordinator and get something on tape." He responded rather doubtfully with, "Maybe," then he was quiet the rest of the way home.

That night I sent Linda an email before scouring the message boards for transports that we could possibly include in our documentary.

Hi Linda!

Before I go to bed I'd like to let you know how much fun it was to transport Blondie. She is more beautiful and cuddly than I ever imagined. They seemed to have taken very good care of her on the transport. And what a darling little sweater someone gave her!

Jessa was, well, speechless when I placed Blondie in her arms. She seemed so happy, and we met her husband too. Thank you for all you sent along in such an organized fashion.

Let's hope all goes well with little Blondie's health from here. She's home in Maine by now, hopefully all comfy and sleeping soundly.

Now you can get some sleep too Linda!

Take care,

Bonnie

Linda replied the next day ...

She is truly a little sweetheart...I'm so glad I could be part of getting her to her "fur-ever" home. We had a terrible time finding a sweater for her - the stores had hardly any left - and nothing between small and extra large - so there wasn't much choice...but I thought the collar was classy and she has such a pretty face.

She will outgrow it in a heartbeat but we had such warm weather here lately and she was going so far north that I just didn't want to take

a chance with her short hair keeping her warm
enough.

She loves the squeaky toys, and the rope was to
try to get her to chew on thick things instead
of cords.

I'm going to miss that little one...with
training, this pup will grow to be a wonderful
dog and a joy to her family for the rest of
her life.

Linda

Transport coordinators are in great demand, as anyone who scans
the animal rescue and transport message boards knows. It seems that
there are many more requests for coordinators than there are volunteers available to perform this remarkable task.

If I were a rescued dog needing to travel from my foster family's
home to my forever home, I would want a woman named Terri Epp
to coordinate my transport.

Terri volunteers her time, lots of time, to help save animals she
never sees. She works efficiently and non-pretentiously from her
home in Ontario, where she can be found moving animals all over
the map of the United States and sometimes across two bordering
countries.

Her transports appear frequently on the message boards. During
the week, she posts her polite, no-nonsense requests for drivers willing to take on the responsibility of chauffeuring creatures of every
age, size, and breed. On the weekends, Terri monitors the journeys
of these animals as they make their
way to rescues and foster or adoptive homes.

What struck me about Terri
was her ability to simultaneously
monitor three to five transports
at a time. Some of her transports
have multiple animals on the jour-

Terri and cat.

ney. Some require overnight stays. Others have complex routes. A few need to be cancelled and posted all over again.

Her task is a daunting one, requiring patience, skill and diplomacy. So how does she do it?

> *Without the internet, I would not be able to do this because I'm dealing with people who are in another country in most cases, and there is a fair amount of communication back and forth. The way this is done is through Yahoo! Groups, so without the ability of the internet, I wouldn't be able to find or talk to these people.*

I asked Terri if she could brief me on exactly what a Transport Coordinator does.

> *I set up transports. First I look at where I'm coming from and going to, and then I sit down with my Rand-McNally paper map and visualize where I'm going. And usually I plan out the route doing it that way, and then I sit down with a mapping program on the computer to figure out the length of time and the mileage. Then from there, I type the actual transport out.*
>
> *The legs of a transport refer to the distance between Point A and Point B – for instance you'll have a driver going from Baltimore, Maryland, to Wilmington, Delaware. That would be considered one leg of a transport. It's usually one or two hours one-way for the volunteer driver.*
>
> *The trips are moderated by me via telephone so the day of the transport, as soon as a driver has completed their portion of the trip, they call me on the phone and just let me know that everything went fine.*
>
> *They let me know if it's moving on time, or if it's behind or ahead of schedule so I can let the other drivers know what is happening. I also ask about the health of the dogs– are they sick or are they acting okay on the transport so that any additional information I'm able to pass on to the drivers.*

I wondered how the animals dealt with these trips – all the strangers, riding along in vehicle after vehicle, overnight stays in unfamiliar settings, new sights, new smells, new sounds...

In most cases, they actually do quite well. The drivers are usually very loving and considerate. Most of them bring a passenger along who cuddles them and talks to them, or if they're in a crate, just make sure that they're comfortable within their crate.

They supply the animal with water along the way, and take them for walks in-between each leg of the transport. It depends mostly on temperament, age and health: some dogs are more nervous and they will find it more stressful; other dogs are very laid back and easy-going and love to go on car trips, so they have no problem at all.

I think that these animals in some cases know they're going to a better place. They definitely know that along the way there's someone caring for them and just providing them with attention and, especially when they're coming from a shelter, I think they have to know they're going to a better place.

A few of the transports I saw posted on the message boards required twenty-something legs spanning a three-day trip. I asked Terri if she thought some of these transports were too long, and too much to ask of an animal.

I do think that in some cases the trips can be too long for an animal. Again, it depends on the animal's age, health and temperament. If it's an animal who is quite ill, and there is actually a rescue or someone closer by, it's always best to find the closest person or adopter that is going to take care of this animal in a good way versus sending it the greater distance.

Now sometimes there is no choice – the dog has to go somewhere for a medical purpose to get proper vetting, and in that case you just have to make sure that they're as comfortable as possible, and as well taken care of as possible.

Really the only other option other than doing a ground transport for some of these animals is to fly them, which is incredibly expensive and also is not necessarily wonderful for their health due to weather in the cargo department.

I wanted to know what had happened since gas prices rose. Has the cost of filling up had an affect on filling the legs of a transport with volunteers?

Yes, it has. The volunteers are not only volunteering their time, they're also volunteering their gas, and the wear and tear on their vehicle. So when gas prices took a big jump, many of the volunteers either decided that whereas in most cases they'd been doing transports every weekend, they were now going to reduce it to perhaps one or two a month, or they were saying, "Okay, I will take a hundred dollars each month and donate it towards transport," but it has caused many people to have to budget their volunteering in the area of transport.

And what if all the legs of the trip aren't filled with volunteers by your departure date?

I always try to go above and beyond to be sure I can get it filled, but in some cases, depending on what geographic region you're going through, there may be very few people who drive, and in those cases if the transport needs to be cancelled we reschedule for the following weekend, or sometimes a dog may be able to get onto another transport that's already traveling in that direction.

I wondered if Terri's transport coordinating was a service she provided exclusively for canine and feline travelers.

No, it isn't just limited to dogs and cats. I have transported rabbits before. At this point, I've never done birds or anything of that nature but I have transported rodents.

The more I talked with Terri, the more I wished I could sit with her at length over afternoon tea. Her sincerity, warmth, and good humor were infectious. It didn't surprise me to learn that her superhero transport escapades were set in motion by a rescued dog.

I started transporting in 2001 after I had adopted a rescued Dachshund of my own named Moose from Dachshund Rescue North America. He came to me through this process, and I asked the person who had coordinated it for my dog, "How can I get involved?"

And she said they're always looking for people to coordinate transports. So I had her show me once or twice and it seemed to click, and I've been doing it ever since. I've taken some breaks over the years, but in general I probably do anywhere from three to five a weekend.

I guess I continue to volunteer because I enjoy it, number one. It's something that I'm able to do here from my home, and I have two small boys so I don't have to leave my house to do it. I can get on the computer for a few moments and if my children need me I can leave and come back.

I enjoy knowing that I'm assisting animals either to get to a rescue or to their new home. Again, I enjoy the fact that it's a volunteer effort I can do right from my home. I don't have to find someone to watch my children while I do it, I can continue to care for them and set up transports. It just gives a good feeling to know that you're doing something for animals.

I knew that Terri rarely had the opportunity to touch or hold any of the animals she listed as passengers on her transport run sheets. I wondered if she ever received photos of the precious cargo in her care.

Yes, I do. The drivers are wonderful about sending along pictures and stories, and if someone has overnighted, they'll send like a little diary entry of how the overnight went, so the drivers are very committed to letting me know what is happening, and to make sure I receive pictures.

Terri Epp
Transport Coordinator
Board Member, Canadian Yorkshire Terrier Rescue

Lynnette Spratley provided overnight accommodations and more for a dog aboard one of Terri's transports.

> When a call went out for someone to help get a found Dachshund to the vet so he could later be transported across the country to a foster home, I responded quickly. The dog was in Pooler, GA, which happens to be where I work, and also where my vet is.

> The Dachshund, dubbed Oscar by the family that found him tied to a telephone pole and abandoned, would be traveling from Georgia to his new foster home in Louisiana. I also offered to take the first leg of the transport.
>
> The family who brought Oscar in from the cold thought he might be a puppy, but

Oscar.

> it turns out he is simply small and somewhat ignorant of what living in a home is really like.
>
> I picked up Oscar on a Thursday and took him for his rabies shot. He was frightened and shaky at first. He spent the afternoon in my office, which is very small, and he soon settled down enough for a nap. He was very quiet and undemanding, but seemed to appreciate a bite of deli ham from my sandwich.
>
> We weren't sure how Oscar would react to my other dogs, nor to my cat. He wagged his tail at the dogs and ignored the cat completely. Seems Oscar was more interested in the food brought home by my husband, who works in a barbecue restaurant. Oscar adores scraps. No, Oscar worships scraps.

He was extremely receptive to both my husband and my stepson (who not only took the first legs of transport, but kept Oscar overnight on Friday), but whenever I moved too suddenly or spoke too loudly, Oscar instantly dropped to his belly on the floor, as if to make himself small and unnoticeable. Still, he was happy to sleep in my lap while I watched television.

We have no idea what Oscar went through before he was rescued, other than that we suspect it was far from pleasant. Yet, whatever horrors humans put this little dog through, Oscar is willing to give us all another chance.

He's one of the sweetest dogs we've ever met. My husband was upset that I didn't ask if we could keep Oscar permanently. And on Saturday, after Oscar had been handed off to transporters from Atlanta, my stepson confided that his wife was also upset. She wanted to keep Oscar forever, too!"

Lynnette Spratley, Volunteer

I was duly impressed by Terri's ability to do what she does while caring for two small children. I marveled even more when she shared something of a personal nature – her struggles on behalf of her youngest son.

Her tow-headed tot is unable to walk, and Terri spends many hours in medical offices trying to find out why, while advocating for the best possible services available to help her little boy.

◆◆◆

Surprisingly, we were finally granted permission to ride along and tape a transport, reality style! The approval came from Carolyn Fitzgerald in Mooresville, North Carolina. Her Maine Coon Rescue had some little Maine Coon cats who needed to get from their foster Mom in Connecticut to an adopter in Maine.

Russ called Sam and asked if he was willing to ride in the transport vehicle with a first-timer and two twelve-week-old kittens.

Our plan was to drive alongside him in the chase vehicle until we met the transfer at a rest stop in Maine.

Sam, who was by nature a patient, animal-loving guy, knew that we were desperately in need of transport footage. He also knew that I was very partial to *his* footage, and his ability to instinctively frame up and capture exactly what was needed to tell a story.

He had remained on stand-by for weeks, checking in periodically to find out if we could meet up with drivers and roll tape. He never lost faith in the project, though he could have just as easily abandoned it and walked away.

As transport after transport turned us down or got cancelled, I became more and more concerned. I knew that Sam had an upcoming commitment with the New England Patriots, and we were running out of time. Sam told Russ he was "in" for the kitten transport and I breathed a huge sigh of relief. If this run could go smoothly, then surely we would be welcomed by other transport coordinators engaged in moving dogs, cats, rabbits, and perhaps even larger animals to where they would be safe.

Stacy Schall, who had been briefed in advance about the production's mission, was "on" from the moment we met up with her. She arrived chauffeured by her boyfriend Brandon, whom she had cajoled into driving to Maine. With two first-time transporters, two kittens, and a first-class camera operator, we were on the road and finally taping what I wanted to share with the world.

When Sam asked Stacy if rising gas prices could effect her volunteering, she sounded like she'd been doing this for years…

> *I know gas prices are getting a little bit more expensive, but when you think about it, what's ten dollars in gas to save these two kittens' lives? So it's really a no-brainer for us.*
>
> Stacy Schall

The kittens were fast asleep, all curled up in the comfort of one another. I thought about what Stacy had said. *A ride? Was that really all that stood between death and freedom for these innocent, tiny animals?*

I asked Stacy and Brandon how the kittens, whose names were Michael and Chester, had fared thus far on the trip.

Michael did get a little bit sick in the litter box on the way up, probably nerves, probably a little bit anxious being away from his mother.

Stacy Schall

Stacy will peek her head in and ask "How are you doing, and are you guys okay?" And they'll start meowing, so other than that, if they're not sleeping, they're meowing.

Brandon Cloutier

We watched the tapes during dinner. The weather had cooperated, the transporters were great, and the transfer went off without a hitch. Sam's footage was crisp, magical, full of heart. The kitten transport scenes were a testament to his mastery of the craft.

Yes, we were stalled on Route 95 South for two hours heading home, but Stacy's exuberance spilling over into our viewing room made it all worthwhile. I scribbled "keeper" next to the time code numbers as our first-time transporter spoke…

I'm definitely going to continue transporting as often as I possibly can.

Today we did kittens, next week I'm actually set up to do Mini-Dachshunds.

I'm bringing them directly to their new parents, so I can't wait to see just the happiness on the new parents' faces when they get their new puppies.

Stacy Schall

"That's what we need," Russ said out of context while scanning the road footage. "See if someone will let us ride along with some puppies. And they have to be awake," he added with a smile.

Chapter Six

ALL ANIMALS
BIG AND LITTLE

Annette King-Tucker was one of the people I met purely by chance in cyberspace. She had written a poem that resonated with the animal rescue community, and her name came up again when I was researching parvo, the dreaded puppy virus.

She had participated in a canine parvo study since its beginnings, and told me how her parvo recovery rate had jumped to one hundred percent with the aid of the drug Tamiflu. Her youngest canine to recover was a four-day-old bottle fed Miniature Pinscher pup.

The multitude of animals, including birds, both wild and domestic, that Annette had rescued or assisted was astonishing. Her archived photos of some of the creatures treated at her ranch included dogs, squirrels, Cotton Tail rabbits, an American Bittern, lambs,

Annette King-Tucker and Kiara.

raccoons, owls, moles, Peacocks, a Mallard duck, a fox, armadillos, a bear, a kangaroo, and a cougar whom she referred to as her best friend.

> *Kiara, an abused cougar, was an illegal pet, confiscated by Fish and Game and sent here. Her front claws and her baby canine teeth removed with wire cutters (home job,*

no anesthesia or anesthetic) she was a mess of pain and infection, unable to walk or eat.

Kiara came to me a starving, aggressive, angry cat, weighing less than forty pounds, and today (six years later) is nearly three hundred pounds of happy, purring, slobbering, affectionate lap kitty.

Though the de-claw severed the front tendons in her feet, Kiara is doing very well and is healthy and so far isn't in any pain because of it.

She is my best friend and truly a rescue I thank God that I was asked to perform…proof that even the most battered of souls can love and trust again.

Annette King-Tucker
Wild Heart Ranch Wildlife Rescue
Claremore, OK

Wire cutters, which had caused Kiara so much excruciating pain, would later aid Annette in alleviating an animal's misery.

Today a call came in from a man I didn't know. He said he had picked up a wolf hybrid along the road. She was dragging a steel cable. He loaded her in his truck and discovered she was wearing a choke chain imbedded over two inches deep inside most of her neck.

He started calling around for help. He couldn't find any. He called me. I called around. Nothing. I spoke to Animal Control while he was there with the officer. She said the wolf needed to be put down. I arranged euthanasia with Doctor Cash.

I again spoke to the animal control officer. She went on about how beautiful and how sweet the wolf was. My guts ached. She had survived the worst of this. How could I request her death now that she was finally getting help?

I again spoke to the man. I asked him if he would be willing to drive all the way out to me for the chance that I may be able to help her. If her injury was over my head, he *would have to take her back to town to be put down. He said he would be happy to bring her to me.*

They arrived shortly. I climbed into the back of his truck. What I saw I will never forget. A choke chain was cut through every bit of muscle around her neck and her flesh had grown through the links of the chain. I was **furious!**

I ran to the house and got wire cutters. When I got back to the truck the man told me they had already tried that. "Yeah, but I haven't!!!"

I cut the chain at the main link and bent it with my super human **"I'm so mad I could do anything right now"** *strength.*

I then gently began to tediously remove the steel from this poor animal's flesh. (Keep in mind I am working on a strange and stray wolf that, standing, is well above my waist.) She never moved, never fought, never flinched. She knew exactly what I was doing for her.

When it finally released her, I flung it like it had burned me. I was sick. The smell of her rotting neck nearly knocked me out, but I hugged her and loved her anyway. Amazingly, she loved me back.

Once inside I fed her everything on the shelves that looked like steak on the can. I got out my best comforters for the most sore of pups. She is nothing

Koda's wounds.

but bones. I don't know why she is alive, but she is not only alive, she is energetic and happy, even playing with me.

In a month, it will only be a story of one I loved and cared for, and the evidence of the crime will be gone. Today she is my whole world. I think that forever if I am asked what was my greatest moment, I will answer, "Taking a chain off a wolf." She is special. So very special.

Koda today.

I just can't express it.

Chains are for gates, for towing cars, for securing loads...Chains are not and never will be for a dog. Never, ever, and never. It is an outrage.

Look into the face of this incredible animal. She is an absolute sweetheart. Anyone could approach her. Thank God for the man that picked her up today. Why did it take so long?

I Am An Animal Rescuer

I am an Animal Rescuer
My job is to assist God's creatures
I was born with the need to fulfill their needs
I take in new family members without plan, thought, or selection
I have bought dog food with my last dime
I have patted a mangy head with a bare hand
I have hugged someone vicious and afraid
I have fallen in love a thousand times
and I have cried into the fur of a lifeless body

I have animal friends and friends who have animal friends
I don't often use the word "pet"
I notice those lost at the road side
And my heart aches
I will hand raise a field mouse
And make friends with a vulture
I know of no creature unworthy of my time

I want to live forever if there aren't animals in Heaven
But I believe there are
Why would God make something so perfect and leave it behind
We may be master of the animals,

But the animals have mastered themselves
Something people still haven't learned

War and abuse makes me hurt for the world
But a rescue that makes the news gives me hope for mankind
We are a quiet but determined army
And making a difference every day

There is nothing more necessary than warming an orphan
nothing more rewarding than saving a life
No higher recognition than watching them thrive
There is no greater joy than seeing a baby play
who only days ago, was too weak to eat

I am an Animal Rescuer
My work is never done,
My home is never quiet
My wallet is always empty
But my heart is always full

– Annette King-Tucker

Things were beginning to change. Coordinators were contacting us on their own with elaborate itineraries perpared for animals who otherwise were doomed. My excitement was hard to contain once I received word of a transport leaving Baton Rouge, Louisiana, with four rescued rabbits. These lucky bunnies would be transported, cared for, and handed off by a finely tuned team of bunny lovers all the way to Roseville, California.

The Coordinator for the Great Bunny Transport, Jennifer Barbieri, offered some background on herself and her long-eared passengers.

> In 2002 I joined a rabbit rescue in Philadelphia. I wasn't aware until then the staggering numbers of rabbits euthanized in shelters. Rabbits are the third most popular pet in the U.S. after dogs and cats, and many shelters are not educated and equipped to handle rabbit adoptions.

Rabbits are very unique pets. They are very smart and sociable animals who do well living inside with family members. I have six rescued/rehomed rabbits who love to play and tease myself, my husband, and each other.

When I watch them play (and even outsmart me on occasion) I can't help but think how someone was eager to give them up. Having six rabbits at home is a lot of work and although I would love to save them all, I do my part by transporting homeless rabbits to better places.

RabbitWise's Bunderground Railroad (aka RW BGRR) is a resource tool for rabbit rescuers making emergency placements and travel arrangements for rabbits in need.

My official role in RW BGRR is Head State Coordinator. I am responsible for overseeing the day-to-day operations of the group and the coordinating of interstate transports with the State Coordinators.

We have had many kinds of animal lovers help us transport rabbits. Our transporters have mostly been rabbit owners or members of local rabbit rescues.

Bunnies on Board

The five rabbits scheduled to be transported from Baton Rouge, Louisiana, to Roseville, California, were housed in a barn with fifty to sixty other rabbits. The owner had a rabbitry that showed rabbits at local fairs. A month after Hurricane Katrina, another storm hit the area and a nearby tree hit the roof of the barn the rabbits were in.

The damage to the barn was substantial and several cages were crushed. A couple of rabbits died. The remaining rabbits in the crushed cages were then placed in cages with other rabbits.

The overcrowding was intense, and the owner agreed to place some of the rabbits elsewhere. A kind lady nearby stepped in to help. She facilitated the release of the five rab-

bits. *The owner since decided to stop breeding the rabbits and is now allowing the local SPCA to help adopt them out.*

These rabbits who have been affected by post Hurricane Katrina events have affectionately been dubbed the "Katrina Rabbits."

Jennifer Barbieri
Head State Coordinator
RabbitWise's Bunderground Railroad

No Room at Local Animal Inns

Jennifer explained that the five rabbits were fairly young, between six months and two years old, and in relatively good health. There were two New Zealand rabbits, one female and one male; and three dwarf rabbits, one female and two males. All of the rabbits had white fur and red eyes. It seemed the rabbits had to travel an incredibly long distance to receive the care they needed. I wondered if the trip would make them ill, or even kill them.

According to Jennifer, the already traumatized rabbits had no choice but to make the lengthy trek. Local resources were overloaded with Katrina animal victims. No one could take in any more.

Melanie Giroir, who helped facilitate the release of the five rabbits, was the first to comment from Louisiana as the Great Bunny Transport sprouted wings.

I am totally amazed how so many people from so many different locations were able to get this transport on the road. Most of us have never seen each other, only talked on the phone or email.

It is so satisfying to know that there are people out there that care deeply enough to sacrifice their personal time, vehicle and gas money to help one another with the same mission – helping animals in need. Thank you everyone!

Melanie Giroir and her personal bunny crew

Leg One Gets Underway

Tani Legleu had the honor of driving the first leg of the long journey west. She reported back to Jennifer, her Transport Coordinator, once the five bunnies had left overcrowded accommodations and showbiz behind:

```
From: Tani
Sent: Saturday, February 11, 2006 1:18 pm
To: Jennifer
Subject: Re: Thank you

Well, let's see:

I picked up the rabbits from the veterinar-
ian/owner, Dr. B., around 1pm. There were five
rather than the four I expected, which was good
since she is trying to reduce her show stock to
a more manageable number.

They were beautiful white rabbits that seemed
to be albinos by the eye color. I'm not an ex-
pert though so she explained that is typical
of New Zealand Whites. They were very calm. I
guess they are used to travel if they are show
rabbits.

Dr. B. didn't seem particularly happy or sad
to see them go. From what I know of her, she
is rather practical and maybe not too attached
emotionally to them or maybe she is just not
one to show emotion after so many years as a
vet.

She had sent along plenty of hay and pellets
and fresh vegetables and even a cooler with
freezer packs to keep them in. She also needed
the cages back, so had sent along mailing la-
bels and her contact number and was planning to
pay to ship the cages back after the rabbits
arrived at their destination.

We drove two hours to Lake Charles, fighting
high gusty cross-road winds between Lafayette
```

and LC in my ancient 18-year-old Camaro (they wouldn't fit in the other car, a Miata), but she was a trooper and we had no trouble with the car.

The rabbits seemed unfazed, but as expected, did not eat much. I guess they will settle down and eat and drink once they get to their over-night accommodations in Houston.

We met up with Renee in LC and switched the guys (and girls) to her SUV. First we stacked the cages in the back so Renee could take a picture of me with the buns, and then we moved them to the back seat behind her and handed out clumps of hay for them to eat before hitting the highway again.

We petted them a little and they mostly seemed to enjoy that. Unfortunately, we discovered a rather large (maybe penny sized) bite wound on one that seemed to be partially healed.

I suggested they call or take her to the vet in the morning since it didn't appear to need urgent care and see if they could possibly put Neosporin or some other antibiotic/disinfectant on it. I'm sure it will heal just fine.

Good luck little buns! I hope you have no trou-ble finding happy homes in your new state.

Tani Legleu
Capital Area Animal Welfare Society (CAAWS)

The Meaning of Rescue

Renee Brennan, a first-time transporter who sings for "animal au-diences only," was incredibly well-prepared. I learned something in-teresting from peeking in on Renee's notes. Dogs may need to stretch their legs after a long ride, but rabbits stretch something else.

The day before my leg of the Bunderground Railroad transport I began to prepare for picking up the four bunnies. I cleaned out the Expedition, and not knowing the size of the cages they would be in, I decided to take the larger of our SUVs.

I packed some parsley, Oxbow hay (my bunny, Jelly Bean's favorite), small bowls for water, paper towels, chewy sticks, and some litter material to freshen their litter boxes.

This was my first transport, so I was excited to be involved in such a compassionate mission to get these four bunnies moved from Baton Rouge, Louisiana, to Roseville, California, where they would have a permanent home.

I left my house on Friday, February 3, 2006, around noon and headed to Lake Charles, Louisiana, to meet Tani from Capital Area Animal Welfare Society "CAAWS" located in Baton Rouge. Tani and I planned to meet at a Wal-Mart store parking lot at 3:30 p.m., in Lake Charles. Tani had mentioned that she would be driving her other car, a 1987 Camaro, and was a little worried about the reliability. She knew there was no way that the bunny cages would fit in her 2002 Miata.

A few minutes before we both arrived at Wal-Mart, we spoke on the phone and I asked Tani about the cages the bunnies were in. I had never been involved in a transport before, and I was a little worried about having enough room for four cages. I knew there were no bonded pairs, and assumed they would be in individual cages.

Tani told me we don't have four bunnies, we have five, and there were three in a cage divided by two panels, and the other two bunnies were in a separate cage divided by one panel. I thought, "Wow, sounds like a good setup, I just hope they fit in the back of my Expedition."

When I saw Tani pull up in her Camaro hatchback, I knew if she could get them in her car, I would have no problem at all. I finally got to meet Tani, a real animal person (my favorite kind of people).

As she gave me some information about the bunnies, we started to unload them from her car into mine. My mood began to change. The cages were not at all what I expected.

Tani said, "I know, they look like breeder cages." I climbed in the back of the SUV facing these five rabbits and all of a sudden I understood why this is called a "rescue." It was incredibly sad to see these five white rabbits so cramped in their tiny spaces.

One of the rabbits tried to turn around and he got stuck. I had to open the cage and finish turning him around. Next, I noticed none of them had litter boxes in their space because there was no room.

As Tani headed back for Baton Rouge, and I headed for the gas station, I was feeling really bad for these bunnies. I filled up the car with gas, pulled the car over and climbed in the back again to face the rabbits.

I had to tell them how sorry I was that humans did this to them. As I started to cry they all just looked at me like they were so interested to hear what else I had to say.

As I petted each one of the rabbits, I tried to reassure them that from now on they don't have to be afraid of humans, and the people they are about to meet have been waiting and planning to make a happy life for them…the way it should have always been. They looked at me like they understood everything I said.

I assumed they were probably hungry so I gave them some water, Oxbow hay, parsley and some chewy sticks. I had to break some of the sticks because I had only planned to have four bunnies.

As I climbed back into the driver seat getting ready to leave the gas station parking lot, I turned back again to see the bunnies and I knew these poor deprived bunnies had never eaten "Oxbow hay." They were munching so fast, I had to give them more. They loved the stuff!

As I was getting back on the highway heading to the Houston area, I called my husband, Tom, (aka Jelly Bean's dad), and asked him to go to the Bunderground Railroad forum to update everyone and let them know the bunnies would be crossing the Texas State line shortly, and that we now have five bunnies instead of four.

I had previously planned on entertaining the bunnies by singing to them on the trip to Houston. I sing to all of my animals.

A few days before the transport, Jan from BGRR had mentioned the song "Little Rabbit Foo Foo" and all the words came back to me – so they heard that one probably four times. Then

Tani with the five rescued rabbits.

I station surfed on the car stereo for some easy listening songs, but only the songs that I knew all of the words to.

While singing, I would turn around just to let them know they were special and I was singing to them, and one of the big rabbits on the end, I'm assuming a male, looked at me like "Carry on, I find this very entertaining."

I know people would feel tortured by my singing, but I really do believe the rabbits liked it. They were all puffed out and were beginning to look so relaxed.

While driving to Houston, I think the bunnies and I stopped about three times just so I could open the top of those tiny cages and let them stretch their ears up, instead of flat back.

As we approached Houston, I called Debbie Hanson, another awesome bunny person. She and her husband had the leg from Houston to Dallas, after the bunnies would spend a relaxing night at their house.

Debbie and I had planned on meeting at the Sam's parking lot about 7:15 p.m. I arrived at Sam's a little before Debbie, so I climbed into the back again to say bye to the bunnies, and not to worry because these people LOVE bunny wabbits!

Then Debbie and her husband Hugh drove up. I knew from Debbie's messages on the BGRR that she was a sincere bunny person. Before the transport, she asked all of the detailed questions on the BGRR forum to be sure she was well prepared, and by doing so, she helped me to get prepared. The "perfect bunny Mom," Debbie gets out of her car and she is proudly wearing a t-shirt with a picture of her adorable lop, Pixel.

We walked toward each other and just hugged. This has truly been a journey from start to finish of awesome compassion and love, and I'm so happy to have been a part of it.

Renee Brennan

The Bunnies Meet the Rabbit Whisperer

The next leg of the trip proved to be a turning point for the rabbits. They would be given names, and they would stay overnight with a woman who could both speak and understand the language of bunnies.

Saturday February 4, 2006
Houston, Texas, to Dallas, Texas - 239 miles 4 hours
Debbie Hanson RW Conductor
Houston to Dallas Transporter Log

Friday afternoon on February 3rd, I slammed into high gear getting four pens set up in the upstairs family room. Furniture was rearranged to make room for the mid- to large-size pens. All needed to be cleaned and disinfected although they had been stored in a closet.

Water bowls were also disinfected before being attached to the wire walls. Puppy pads were placed on the floors. Litter boxes were disinfected and filled with bedding and fresh hay. Hoarded cardboard toilet tissue rolls were cleaned and stuffed with hay, one per pen.

A fast run to the grocery store added more Romaine lettuce, lettuce leaf, and Cilantro parsley to our larder. Thinking I was ready for our overnight furry guests, I checked the message board on Rabbitwise's Bunderground Railroad, to find out that I needed to add one more of everything.

A fifth rabbit had been unexpectedly included in the transport. Well, hurray that another bunny would be taken out of a horrendous situation, but I needed to scramble to get ready for it.

About 8:00 p.m. my husband and I met Renee Brennan under the gauzy glare of a gas station on a busy street corner in Houston. She introduced us to our charges. While excited to meet the rabbits, I was horrified by the cages in which the rabbits had been sent.

We transferred the cages, hay, and other supplies from Renee's SUV to ours, said our good-byes, and promised to keep in touch.

On the way home, I stopped at a nearby Petco to price carriers. I could not tolerate the idea of the five rabbits traveling for a week or more in those hell-cages. The two larger rabbits did not have room to turn around, much less sit up. The three smaller rabbits were little better off.

All were crouched on wire floors without room to stretch out. The least expensive carrier Petco had was about $25 and it was smaller than I was comfortable with, although still much larger than the hell-cages. I needed five of them. We'd have to think on this.

My husband took charge of getting the rabbits into their pens. The two larger ones got the two largest pens we had. The three smaller rabbits were then settled into the medium-size pens. This was most probably the most room these rabbits had ever had.

The largest male (I named Pappa) went immediately to the litter box and watched the "goings on" from the comfort of a padded "floor." The largest female (named Mamma) also took comfort in standing on the bedding material in the litter box.

This made perfect sense to me. Their feet must have hurt a great deal from being in a crouch position on the wire floor for twelve hours or more. The smallest male (Eeyore) laid against the pen door where my husband had put him down.

One rabbit was injured (Patton.) He had a large scraped area on his right flank, several smaller scrapes on his shoulder and neck, and scrapes around his eyes. He was, however, interested in exploring his pen.

A very young, thin female (Slim Pickens) was exuberant in exploring her temporary home. The first thing she did was to rearrange the litter box. Obviously I'd placed it in the wrong area (silly human).

We got the rabbits settled in and left them alone for a while to rest. Pappa stayed in the litter box and dozed. Mamma kept an eye on me while she tried to stand on her hind legs to get a better look. Her back legs were not strong enough to support her efforts for long. She seemed incredulous that she had enough room to stretch all the way up and still not hit the ceiling. She just didn't know there was so much room in the whole world!

Eeyore eventually crept to his litter box where he rested. Patton was fascinated with the puppy pad on the floor and rearranged it multiple times. Slim Pickens flipped her litter box over, dumping its entire contents onto the floor where it should have been in the first place.

The water bowls were a little confusing at first to the rabbits. But Slim Pickens was the first to investigate her *bowl and quickly the other rabbits caught on that there was water in "them thar bowls." Each water bowl held about eight ounces of water. Each rabbit emptied its bowl by morning. Those were very thirsty rabbits.*

Pappa and Mamma didn't know what the fresh lettuce and Cilantro was for. They found it curious but just didn't understand it. The "young 'uns" however, nibbled, then scarfed down the fresh vegetables.

Room to roam.

Everybody was familiar with pellets, however, and ate their fill. Slim Pickens discovered that if she grabbed the puppy pad between her teeth and stood on it, she could tear it! It made the most wonderful ripping sound! Then she'd look up at me with a grin on her face and ask, "Is that not the coolest sound you've ever heard?" I had to admit that it was, indeed, the coolest sound I'd ever heard.

Lights were turned off for the night and I slipped into the computer room, still fretting over the hell-cages the rabbits had been traveling in. I was determined that if it was at all feasible, those cages would go no further.

I checked the Wal-Mart website and they had carriers for fifteen dollars each. It was a possibility. I also emailed the Houston SPCA, explained the situation, and asked if they would donate five carriers for the rabbits.

One last look at the bunnies before I headed to bed at about 3:00 a.m. Saturday morning. Pappa was stretched full out on his side at the front of his pen. I do believe I heard him snoring softly.

Mamma was stretched out but came quickly alert when I entered. I apologized for disturbing her. Eeyore was hidden between his litter box and the back of the pen, just showing me an eye and an ear.

Patton was asleep in front of his litter box with the puppy pad bunched up around him. Slim Pickens was stretched out with her feet fully extended behind her in a most unladylike position. She didn't care. Neither did I.

I couldn't sleep. I kept thinking about the hell-carriers. I just couldn't put those wonderful personalities back into those small torture chambers. Just couldn't do it. There was such an aura of peace, gratitude, and relief about them that needed to remain.

With Saturday's dawn, I was adamant that we wouldn't use the hell-carriers. We fed the rabbits again, and gave everyone a refill in their water bowls. Then I checked my email, and the Houston SPCA had responded that they would certainly donate the carriers and whatever else we needed.

However, time was against us. It would take a minimum of three hours to make the round trip to the SPCA, including getting the carriers, etc. My husband and I decided to check Wal-Mart first. The closest store to us had four carriers. I bought all four of them. We then went to another Wal-Mart further away and bought one more carrier.

We had our five carriers, and were two hours behind schedule. We should have been almost halfway to Dallas by now. Sarita was expecting us about one o'clock.

We loaded our SUV with hay and supplies. When it came time to move the rabbits from the pens to the carriers, the only rabbit that voiced its opinion was Patton. He was not inclined to leave his pen. Actually, he was having "none of it!"

He vigorously displayed his displeasure by squirming and lunging to get away from my husband's firm grasp. "Don't put me back in dat bad cage! I not going! I staying here! Dis is a guud place and I'm staying!"

My husband got both hands around Patton, lifted him out of the pen, and set him down immediately in front of the carrier door. Patton inspected the carrier. My husband gave Patton a moment. Patton stretched toward the interior.

My husband patted Patton's little bunny butt and Patton hopped into the carrier. While the door was secured, Patton looked out at us. "Well, you didn't tell me dat you gotted us mansions to travel in! Dis is very okay!"

We loaded the rabbits up and headed for Interstate Highway 45 toward Dallas, three hours late. When we were about halfway to Dallas, I called Sarita and gave her the "low down."

She was not aware that a fifth rabbit was coming her way. She was glad for the "heads up" so she could get a fifth pen ready. I told her about the carriers, but I'd forgotten water bottles. She'd be happy to get them.

We had a rest stop at Woody's in Centerville. Expecting the rabbits to be stressed and upset we were surprised to find them quite calm. Most of them had been using the time to rearrange the puppy pads and eat hay. Pappa, however, had left his puppy pad in place and had spent his time happily snoozing.

Incredible as it seems, the rabbits were in better spirits, more curious, and more rested than they'd been that morning. It was as if they couldn't understand their good fortune, but were determined to enjoy it as long as it lasted. Their aura of gratitude was palpable.

The only dissention among the "troops" was to comment on my husband's driving with "thumps." They didn't seem to appreciate his rather quick stops and sharp turns!

Sarita met us in her driveway about four o'clock Saturday afternoon. We got Pappa, Mamma, and Eeyore settled in with Sarita and her herd of rabbits.

Sarita has several personal rabbits and several more fosters, all of whom are beautiful, healthy rabbits. I showed Patton's injuries to Sarita. She, too, was concerned about them. Sarita picked Slim Pickens up for an inspection and Slim cuddled into Sarita's lap quite happy to be held and petted.

For all of Slim Pickens' "goofyness" she is a most loving and snuggly bunny, which is very unusual for rabbits. Normally, rabbits want "four on the floor!" They do not want to be picked up. But Slim Pickens was soaking up the love, comfort, and security that Sarita so freely offered her.

Patton found that he could lift the puppy pad, throw it into the air with his nose, get under it, and it would float down onto him. Then he would toss it a little, just enough to get his head out, and look up at us with a grin.

The gratitude emanating from these rabbits was incredible. To see them snuggle and play was a wonderful sight. It's a memory that still makes me cry. They had such horrible, cold lives, but could still trust. They could still find joy. And, they were infinitely grateful for the little bit of kindness we could offer.

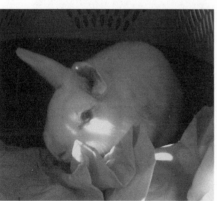

My husband and I drove back to Houston that same day, arriving about 9:00 p.m. I climbed the stairs to the family room and

Traveling in style.

was met with five pens. Hay, poop, pee, pieces of vegetables, and pellets everywhere waiting for me to clean it up. Not a puppy pad still in place. Even though I was physically and emotionally exhausted, my first thought was, "I miss them!"

It's been close to six weeks since we had our five guests for a single night, and still, I miss them.

Debbie Hanson
Houston RW Conductor

Two More First-Timers Heard From

10:00 am to 11:30 am (CST)
Ardmore, Oklahoma, to Norman, Oklahoma, 82 miles
Kathy Barton

I was fortunate enough to transport all the bunnies from Ardmore, Oklahoma, to Norman, Oklahoma. It was my first time to transport rabbits, but not my last. As we loaded each into my car, they would curiously come to the front of their carrier.

It was so heartwarming to know they were safe and on their way to such a better life. I'm so honored I could help make this happen.

Kathy Barton

The grateful bunnies were handed off to yet another first-time transporter. Jeanette used the long drive to contemplate some of the rewards of transporting rescued rabbits.

11:30 am to 1:30 pm (CST)
Norman, Oklahoma, to Elk City, Oklahoma, 130 miles
Jeanette Doty from Heartland Rabbit Rescue

This was my first experience in transporting – and what an experience it was! Getting five rabbits from Baton Rouge, Louisiana. all the way to Roseville,

California, is immensely complicated, and I am proud to have had a small part in it.

We had thought that this experience might be an opportunity to be in touch with other organizations, but I did not realize quite how true that would be. Before the rabbits even left Baton Rouge, there were flurries of phone calls and emails keeping everyone informed, asking and answering questions.

On Sunday, February 5th, I met Kathy, the transporter from Ardmore, and we moved the five rabbits in their carriers from her vehicle to mine. We briefly checked on each one, and I handed out paper rolls stuffed with Timothy hay.

I then drove from Norman to Elk City – about 140 miles – and met Vicky and her husband, who were taking the rabbits on to Amarillo. In Elk City, we took some time out to check on each rabbit, provide fresh bedding, add hay, and offer water-drenched greens.

Both Kathy and Vicky are experienced transporters, but had not transported rabbits. I am a complete novice at transporting, but have lived with rabbits for many years.

Under any other circumstances we might not have had a chance to "compare notes." Now I have met at least two other people who care about the well-being of all creatures, and have talked with many more. That is one of the rewards.

Another reward – the rabbits had so little to begin the journey. By the time I got them, they had new carriers, water bottles, hay, food, veggies, water, and bedding. All along their way they were given royal treatment by people who love them without reserve.

And the greatest reward? When I picked up the rabbits, they were still a little frightened and tense. On the way to Elk City, I could hear bunnies chewing and tossing paper rolls. At the Elk City stop, they were beginning to *"claim" their territory, their "stuff" – and be just a bit sassy about it.*

I have heard from others that at each stop the rabbits were more relaxed and comfortable. They know without a doubt that life for them will be all they could hope for.

> Jeanette Doty, President
> Heartland Rabbit Rescue
> Blanchard, Oklahoma

Rescued Rabbits Re-Cap and Run Sheet

Vicky's transport diary included the rabbits' initial itinerary and volunteer drivers. The preliminary run sheet revealed a hole in the transport which, if not filled, could cause an entire trip like the Great Bunny Transport to be cancelled.

1:30 pm to 4:00 pm (CST)
Elk City, Oklahoma, to Amarillo, Texas, 150 miles
Vicky Adams from Pet Helpers

Hi All,

Like a lot of Pet Helpers, I'm on a few lists that share info. on animals. Two of these lists are:

http://groups.yahoo.com/group/I-40_Rescue_and_Transport/

http://groups.yahoo.com/group/OklahomaAnimalRescue/

Around the first of January, I started getting emails asking for volunteers to help a transport coming out of Baton Rouge, Louisiana, going all the way to Roseville, California. Eighteen hundred miles and four bunnies.

They are still finding animals that were either lost or abandoned during the storms. These just happen to be some that would be coming through Western Oklahoma. At the time I didn't know if I could help or not, but I agreed to see what I could do.

I know agreeing to help with something like this is a big commitment. If you back out at the last minute the whole transport could fail. I had faith in the people of Western Oklahoma: I knew if for some reason I couldn't do it, someone else would step forward.

I have great friends and family but sometimes, just like me, they can't volunteer either. Okay, there are always the local radio stations and newspapers, and I was pretty sure they would run a story about bunnies in need, but I wanted to save these resources and not abuse their generosity.

Quite often, transports like this don't succeed, but when they do, a great story unfolds right before your eyes.

Over the next few weeks there were a lot of e-mails and phone calls. Below is one of the e's I got from Jennifer, Head State Coordinator with Rabbit Wise's Bunderground Railroad.

Vicki Adams

Here is the itinerary for the transport of four Baton Rouge Rabbits traveling to Roseville, California. I'm still waiting on info. about the size of the carriers. We'll know for sure tomorrow when Tani picks them up.

Everyone, please look over your contact info. Let me know ASAP if it needs updating. Thank you all for your involvement. Without you, this wouldn't be possible. One last thing, we are still missing the Amarillo, Texas, to Tucumcari, New Mexico, leg. Please forward to anyone you think that may be able to help. I'll keep everyone posted.

Jennifer Barbieri

PRELIMINARY RUN SHEET

Friday February 3, 2006
1:00 pm to 3:30 pm, 128 miles
Baton Rouge, Louisiana, to Lake Charles, Louisiana
Tani from CAAWS

3:30 pm to 5:30 pm, 143 miles
Lake Charles, Louisiana, to Houston, Texas
Renee Brennan from RW BGRR Conductor

Layover in Houston, Texas
Debbie Hanson from RW BGRR Conductor

Saturday February 4, 2006
8:00 am to 1:00 pm, 239 miles
Houston, Texas, to Dallas, Texas
Debbie Hanson from RW BGRR Conductor

Layover in Dallas, Texas
Sarita Rossi from RW BGRR Conductor

Sunday February 5, 2006
8:00 am to 10:00 am, 110 miles
Dallas, Texas, to Ardmore, Oklahoma
Sarita Rossi from RW BGRR Conductor

10:00 am to 11:30 am, 82 miles
Ardmore, Oklahoma, to Norman, Oklahoma
Kathy Barton

11:30 am to 1:30 pm, 130 miles
Norman, Oklahoma, to Elk City, Oklahoma
Jeanette Doty from Heartland Rabbit Rescue

1:30 pm to 4:00 pm, 150 miles
Elk City, Oklahoma, to Amarillo, Texas
Vicky Adams from Pet Helpers

4:00 pm to 6:00 pm, 114 miles
Amarillo, Texas, to Tucumcari, New Mexico
NEEDED

5:00 pm to 7:30 pm, 176 miles
Tucumcari, New Mexico, to Albuquerque, New Mexico
DeAnn Paul from HRS

Layover in Albuquerque, New Mexico
Pam Larsen from Rio Rancho Rabbit Rescue

Monday, February 6, 2006
8:00 am to 10:00 am, 233 miles
Albuquerque, New Mexico, to Holbrook, Arizona
Pam Larsen from Rio Rancho Rabbit Rescue
[RJ - When are you bringing the rabbits to Erika?]

Holbrook, Arizona, to Phoenix, Arizona, 234 miles
RJ from Brambley Hedge Rabbit Rescue

Saturday, February 11, 2006
Phoenix, Arizona, to Los Angeles, California, 389 miles
Erika Royal from Brambley Hedge Rabbit Rescue

```
Jan/Christine/Alinda - forgive me for not fol-
lowing the details of the CA legs. Please fill
me in. Thanks!!
Jennifer
```

Vicky remained concerned about the transport's missing leg...

One thing I want to point out... all of these people are volunteers, no one is being paid to do this, and all volunteers cover the expenses for their leg out of their own pocket. As you can see we are still missing one leg. If it is not filled this transport may not happen.

As you read above, Jennifer asks all of us to cross post this need. I didn't know anywhere else to cross post to. Pet Helpers, Inc. in Western Oklahoma is just getting started. Our network of volunteers is still very small. Who did we know in Amarillo?

Well, Jennifer seemed very confident that the transport would take place...Did she know something I didn't?

Friday Feb. 3rd we were instructed to exchange info with the legs meeting us. That's when I started getting to *know Jeanette Doty from Heartland Rabbit Rescue, www. heartlandrabbitrescue.org*

Cool group...check out their site. Jeanette and I had everything worked out. We would meet in Elk City... Okay, I know how I'm getting the four rabbits, but who am I taking them to?

Friday night when I was getting ready for bed, I was sure the transport would be cancelled. After all, there are a lot more rabbit hunters than rabbit rescuers here.

Saturday morning I checked my e-mail. A transporter for the Amarillo to Tucumcari leg had been found. Diane Trull would be meeting me in Amarillo on Sunday. All I had to do was e-mail her and work out a place to meet.

Though the missing leg had been filled, B-Day was fast approaching, and Vicky still hadn't heard from Diane, a woman who has helped to save thousands of homeless dogs.

Late Saturday afternoon I'm starting to panic. Diane's not answering my e's. Jennifer reassures me that she works on Saturday at a large shelter, with five hundred plus dogs to care for. Diane is a member of Best Friends Network and here's a link to a story about her:

bestfriends.org/allthegoodnews/nmhpnews_080104_dawg.cfm

After pulling this up, I remembered reading about her, and I've been sharing her story with different people for three or more years now. The 4th grade school teacher and her students started a no-kill shelter in the Panhandle of Texas. This is one of my favorite stories on her:

bestfriends.org/allthegoodnews/magazine/dalhart_jan04.cfm

Well sure enough, Diane and I got all the details worked out for Sunday. She would not be meeting me, but her daughter Katie and some young volunteers would.

Sunday, February 5th, B-day is here. Well, before you start patting me on the back for volunteering my time let me explain... I'm also taking my mother to visit her Aunt in the hospital in Amarillo, and I get to see my cousins. My husband agrees to come also, we plan on a little shopping and eating out... you know, make a day of it.

Transports are usually scheduled very tight to be considerate of everyone's time. When we meet there is very little time for talking or anything else. At 1:30 p.m. Jeanette arrived in Elk City, with five white rabbits not four. One more from Louisiana had been added at the last minute and they had luggage, a lot of luggage.

Seems when the bunnies got to Houston they had nothing and were all in one large cage. The Houston group went shopping. Now they each had their own pet taxi, large bag of hay, greens, carrots, puppy pads, toys, all kinds of bunny stuff!

Jeanette gave me a quick lesson on bunny care when transporting, we did a fast cage check and took care of the bunnies' needs. Jeanette is a very knowledgeable lady on rabbits. All pictures taken by 1:55 p.m. and we are on our way to Amarillo.

By 4:15 p.m. we're in Amarillo, and a group of five teenagers pull up in a four-door pickup. It's Katie Trull from Dalhart, Texas. She drove an hour to Amarillo to pick up the bunnies. They loaded the bunnies in the backseat, stacked with two teenagers holding crates, and three riding up front.

By 4:30 p.m. they are on their way to Tucumcari, a two hour drive. They said it would be a one and one-half hour drive back to Dalhart after they drop off the bunnies. See, there are some good teens out there...

Take a little time and get to know some of the people that helped with this, they are great. This was a cool way to spend a Sunday afternoon.

Vicky Adams
Pet Helpers, Inc.
Elk City, Oklahoma

The Leg That Almost Wasn't

Katie Trull and her friends literally went the extra mile and filled the missing leg for the five lucky bunnies, who by now had come to associate the hand-offs with getting new goodies to chew!

4:00 pm to 6:00 pm, 114 miles
Amarillo, Texas, to Tucumcari, New Mexico
Katie Trull from Dalhart Animal Wellness Group & Sanctuary

When we were first contacted to be part of the transport of five rabbits from Louisiana to California, we were somewhat concerned. Our shelter, DAWGS (Dalhart,Texas) has only had exposure to lots of dogs and cats and a few wild animals.

It was our first time to assist in the rescue of beautiful, furry rabbits. We were and are honored to have been part of this great project.

We met the transport at Petsmart in Amarillo, TX. Their vehicle was loaded with rabbit care items. The five rabbits were all beautiful and very inquisitive as to what was going on.

Prior to moving them to the next stop, we cleaned everyone's cages and gave them little puppy pads for the trip. They also got spritzed parsley leaves and fresh water. The previous transfer had given them hay stuffed in toilet paper rolls, which they loved.

We loaded everything onto the back of the truck and carefully placed all of the cages into the vehicle. It was a little cramped with all those nice cages and four adults but we were on the road!

As we drove along, the rabbits nibbled quietly on their toys and seemed quite content. It was as if they knew they were headed to a great place. I was seated in the back seat with them and was slowly being lulled to sleep by the rhythmic chewing and scratching.

My arm slid down next to the opening on one of the cages and I was suddenly jolted awake by the gentle nuz-

zling of the rabbit. She thought she would like to enjoy some of my sweater! Too cute!

Each one of the precious babies is beautiful and so very sweet. When we arrived in Tucumcari, New Mexico, we met the next transfer at Love's. It seemed a fitting place to make the transfer. We quickly loaded them up and sadly said goodbye, wishing them the best on their journey and new homes.

Thank you for including us in your magnificent work and allowing us the opportunity to be part of such a great group that shares a common goal of compassion and caring for the animals.

Most Sincerely,
Katie Trull and friends:
Kathryn Scherer
Meredith Valdez
Tucker Foster
And everyone from DAWGS

DeAnn Paul, who serves as the Development Researcher for the Santa Fe Opera, has been rescuing rabbits for fifteen years. DeAnn's household includes one nine-year-old rabbit, three younger ones, and a Chinchilla she rescued from the Santa Fe Humane Society.

5:00 pm to 7:30 pm, 176 miles
Tucumcari, New Mexico, to Albuquerque, New Mexico
DeAnn Paul

Left Rio Rancho at around two o'clock and headed south to I-40. Weather conditions were slightly cloudy and extremely windy as I drove east on I-40.

About a half an hour from Tucumcari, I received a call from my contacts for the Tucumcari leg. They were running twenty minutes late, so I stopped for gas. When I arrived at our rendezvous spot they were waiting.

As we transferred the buns, they told me one was ill, so I placed this bunny in the front seat with me and the other *four went in the back of the Subaru. Outside of Tucumcari I pulled into a rest stop briefly to re-arrange the bunnies in the back. I moved them closer to the front of the car, where it's less noisy and warmer.*

Again, very windy! I drove up to meet my contact in Albuquerque as she was calling to see where I was and made the transfer.

DeAnn Paul

Layover in Albuquerque, New Mexico
Pam Larsen from Rio Rancho Rabbit Rescue

"Bunny Love"

When Pam Larsen met up with DeAnn and saw the injured rabbit Debbie Hanson had named Patton, it was love at first sight. Pam re-named him Cookie, and adopted him on the spot. The male dwarf had some cuts that were infected, and Pam was committed to nursing him back to health.

Kim DeWoody, who would be taking the rabbits to Roseville, California, and placing them in foster care, was relieved to get the news that one of the rescued rabbits had been adopted. She had originally agreed to secure foster care for four homeless bunnies, and became concerned when she heard five were on their way.

After receiving the bunnies from DeAnn, Pam escorted them to Rio Rancho Rabbit Rescue in Albuquerque for their overnight stay. The next day would be a long day of travel, and everyone needed some rest.

Cookie Postscript

Pam described Cookie's condition upon arrival as "horrible" and would soon discover that he had a Pasteurella infection and a large cyst on his thigh. She connected with someone in Louisiana who was familiar with the rabbits. Pam was told that Cookie was part of a 4-H project that a female vet had going in her yard.

Another bunny transfer.

Despite his traumatic past, Cookie the hurricane survivor thrived and soon had a love interest. Pam described his relationship with Kimo, who was head over feet for Cookie.

He loves his girl, Kimo, who is a mini-Lop mix. She is mean with everyone else but him. They love to cuddle. She puts her head over his back and looks dreamy-eyed.

Pam Larsen

The following morning, Pam drove the four orphan rabbits three and a half hours west to meet Christine.

Monday, February 6, 2006
8:30 am to 12:00 pm, 233 miles
Albuquerque, New Mexico, to Holbrook, Arizona
Pam Larsen from Rio Rancho Rabbit Rescue

I met Pam Larsen in Holbrook and picked up the four bunnies. I gave Pam a carrier I already had from an earlier transport, as it wouldn't fit in my car with the four Katrina rabbits, who had their very own new carriers and I didn't have the heart to switch one out. We met at noon and transferred the rabbits and I hit the road shortly thereafter.

Christine Macey

12:00 pm to 3:30 pm, 239 miles
Holbrook, Arizona, to Kingman, Arizona
Christine Macy, RW BGRR Conductor

The reality of the situation hit me then – I had four precious rabbits in their carriers and it was after noon, and I knew I couldn't make it all the way back. I would be making a stop, and, having four un-bonded, un-neutered rabbits wasn't going to make motel life easy. And, no way would I keep them in carriers overnight. This was not the highlight of my trip.

I stopped in Flagstaff and got directions to a Petsmart and picked up two exercise pens. I already had a baby gate that I'd used overnight for Halo, my earlier one-bunny transport.

I wanted to stop right there and get them set up and relax, but heard on the news the temp would drop into the teens. Being from the balmy climes of Southern California, I did not have antifreeze.

I called my boyfriend who suggested I get somewhere warmer if I ever wanted to be able to get anywhere again in my car, so we had to go on.

Christine Macey

Bunny's Inn

Christine knew of a motel that allowed pets, but would they extend their hospitality to four weary bunnies who had spent the day on the road?

Our night together happened in Kingman, Arizona, where the temps stayed above freezing (mostly) and we got there at a decent hour of the day.

I stayed at a Motel 6 and luckily got a room far from the desk, on the bottom floor with a parking spot in front of the door.

I put the baby gate across the bathroom door making one area. I took a playpen and blocked off the sink and closet space next to the bathroom and could also close that one up to make a pen for another. That made three rabbit spots. I took the last playpen and set it up on the other side of the bed. Now, I had my four rabbit areas.

I had not met these guys yet, but put one carrier in the bathroom and opened the door. This was the little dwarf. The next carrier went into the sink area off the bathroom and I opened that one up and out came the New Zealand youngster.

The playpen that was blocking off her area was for the larger New Zealand mix rabbit; and the one by my bed away from the others was for the adult female who I'd been warned was a bit aggressive. I'd bought three litter boxes at Petsmart and still had one from Halo's transport, so a box went into each spot. Almost done but not quite....

I didn't have bowls for all of them and I needed a dustpan and broom, and right across the street was a K-Mart. You just can't leave a motel room the way this one was already starting to look.

Got home and finally had time to meet them and check sexes, etc. They needed names as it was just too sad for them not to have any, so I tried for Southern ones: Scarlett was the adult female with the rep for being aggressive; Rhett was the adult male; Dixie was the young NZ; and Jackson was the dwarf.

Dixie was already running around like a Banshee and binkying everywhere and I just kept calling her Binkers and that name stuck. Never could refer to her as Dixie.

Binkers looked to be two or three months old and was having a ball. She was nervous to be picked up but when I did she just cuddled forever. I put her down, she hopped away briefly, hopped back, and flopped by my leg. I was hooked.

Rhett, the adult male, was next to her. He was all over his playpen, getting up on his carrier to see what was *going on. He, too, was a lover – very affectionate and oh so happy to be cared for.*

Scarlett, I had learned, was not in the mood to be aggressive. I had already pet her several times when she was in her carrier and she thought that was just fine.

Soon she was out of her carrier and exploring her new spot. In no time at all, I could see she was peeing and pooping just fine.

Little Jackson in the bathroom was another story. I got to him last, probably because getting from my bed into the bathroom was a major undertaking and he was still in his little carrier.

I brought it out and placed it on the bed but he was still not inclined to come out. I let him hang in there for a bit but took him out after awhile to check him over. It dawned on me he might not like the slippery bathroom floor. I got a rug out of the car that I'd used for my easy Halo transport and set it in the bathroom. When I checked on him later, he was out of his carrier, too.

I played with all of them, on the bed and in their playpens. The overwhelming feeling I got from them was one of joy and gratitude. It seemed palpable.

I was very worried about what kind of night we would have when I turned out the light. I had un-neutered bunnies right next to each other and had visions of fighting, etc., through the baby gate or playpen, but they were all well-behaved little rabbits.

Christine Macey

Tuesday, February 7, 2006
Kingman, Arizona, to Bakersfield, California, 335 miles
Christine Macy, RW BGRR Conductor

I hated putting them into their carriers the next morning but they seemed fine with it, and I was able to organize the car this time so that we all fit quite well. We took one break at a rest stop before meeting Jan Davidson in Bakersfield and, I have to say, I didn't want to part with them so soon.

I would have loved to spend another night with them, but it would have been very taxing. It took a good forty-five minutes of being on my hands and knees with the dustpan and whisk broom cleaning up hay and turds from that motel room floor, and there was an element of luck getting a room away from the desk and on ground level. Having to go through it all again would have been the price of getting another night with them.

So, that is the end of this leg of the journey. All I can say is I have never had such a rewarding experience with rabbits, and I've had many encounters. There was something special about all of them, the way they seemed to blossom before my eyes, and the way they seemed genuinely grateful for the basics of rabbit care.

I know they had it rough, all had hock sores and all were urine stained, but all were resilient and learning that there really was a reason to be alive. I will never forget them.

I guess I should also give a word of thanks to my boyfriend Dave. I told him I would be gone for two days, left a note with reminders of how to care for my six rabbits, and had filled the refrigerator with greens. Then I took off for a week. Bless him.

Christine Macey

Are We There Yet?

Finally, the rabbits were given an extended break from traveling and some much-needed R&R. Jan Davidson's four-star bunny hostel included creature comforts like soft sheets, and vegetables they had never seen.

Wednesday and Thursday, February 8 and 9, 2006
2 day layover in Fish Camp, California
Jan Davidson, RW BGRR Conductor

Bright and early on the morning of Tuesday, February 7th, my son Ken and I drove to Bakersfield, California, to meet Christine with the four remaining Katrina rabbits.

We met in some forsaken empty lot east of Bakersfield and had a grand time finally getting to personally see each other. It was a happy occasion, with much hugging, smiles and laughter. (Christine and I had met on the Internet, RW BGRR, and talked for hours on the phone, but never in person.)

Each of the rabbits were taken out, hugged goodbye from Christine, loaded up in my car, and away we all went in our respective directions. The plan was set for the rabbits to have a three-day layover for a much-needed respite after all their days on the road and juggling from place to place. They were incredible little travelers and did marvelously well.

Ken and I got home about four hours later, after dark, and brought everyone in the house. I decided to cordon off the front entrance to our living room and give them a communal, but separated space where they could all see each other.

The enclosures were each about five feet square and set up in a cube shape, where they could all meet at the four corners. Their floor was flannel sheeting, softness I'm sure they'd never before felt under their feet.

Tears came to my eyes as I watched them cautiously come out of their carriers and explore their space. I'm sure they had never seen so much room in their lifetime and we were both so happy for them.

They had fresh water, Timothy hay, fresh greens and small apple slices, along with Timothy pellets. I thought

I could see relief, contentment, and happiness on their sweet faces.

Safe and secure, at long last after who only knows what they had suffered in their past environment.

Next morning they were interested in seeing us, but were quite perplexed at the sight of a carrot (imagine!) and

Rhett explores his new digs.

Rhett, the large male, just chinned his, seemingly not knowing it was something to eat. This made me feel sad, but at the same time I was so happy for him... and his companions. They had fresh salads and all day to enjoy the food and relax.

A time out for Scarlett.

We all became acquainted and began discovering each other's personalities. Rhett, the large male, was totally relaxed and looked as if he had stretched his legs and body as far as he could reach; what a treat to have such space!

He was quite friendly and contactful. Scarlett, the large female, was more apprehensive, but she, too, enjoyed her space. Jackson, the second smallest (male) and most urine stained was very shy and reluctant to come out and explore, but later ventured outside his carrier, though staying close for a quick return inside if necessary.

Binkers, the most petite young female, was a very busy little bunny, hence her name. She was quite delightful, but again, not as contactful as the two larger rabbits.

They were a delight to just sit and watch; pretty much what we did the entire time they were here. Rhett even fell asleep on his back, in my arms, several times.

The entire Wednesday was spent relaxing and becoming comfortable, followed by Thursday when I groomed, cleaned ears, massaged, and examined each one for any potential problems.

During this exam I discovered Jackson had an abdominal mass. It was later diagnosed as an abdominal hernia and surgically repaired during his neuter in Sacramento. Each of the rabbits was gentle, tolerant, and patient during their treatment…

Throughout their entire stay and close contact with each other, not one rabbit bothered the other, nor us. In fact, Rhett spent a lot of time nuzzling up to his and Scarlett's side of their respective enclosure. But never did anyone growl or act aggressive toward his/her companions.

Jan Davidson

Rhett's Rebuttal

It was not an easy day for Jan, Ken, and the four sojourners in their care. One of the bunnies, who may have thought he was finally home, expressed displeasure at being asked to resume his travels.

Friday, February 10, 2006
Fish Camp, California, to Modesto, California, 116 miles
Jan Davidson, RW BGRR Conductor

Friday morning, Feb 10th, was a sad day as we had to pack up and leave. Ken got the car ready, we bundled up all the supplies, put clean litter boxes in the carriers, and began moving each rabbit out.

This was tearing away at both of us emotionally. We had already grown to love each rabbit, each individual and unique personality.

The last rabbit to be placed in his carrier was Rhett, and I wanted to call off the final leg of the transfer when he put his head out, did not want to stay in the carrier, and proceeded to chin my hand. If only I had more space for this family!

Jan and Christine exchange the rabbits.

We drove to Modesto, about three hours north, and met up with Kim DeWoody and her friend Janet at a pre-arranged location. It is interesting how rabbit people manage to spot each other without difficulty; that was the case in this instance.

After much conversation, picture taking, and moving the rabbits into Janet's car, we were all ready to go off, again, in our respective directions.

As Ken and I walked across the parking lot, we both looked over our shoulder, then looked at each other, at which time he said to me, "Are you crying?"

With tears in my eyes, and a heavy heart, I replied, "Yes, and I see you are, too." It was a bittersweet experience.

An aside: I've been involved, fortunately, with rabbits as well as other dear small creatures for many years. But never, in all this time, have I come across rabbits whom both individually and collectively had such incredible karma about them.

There is something very unusual, very special about these rabbits and the way they affected us. I shared this with Christine and she agreed that the same thing had happened with her.

All of us, to this day, are missing these rabbits. The three of us have talked ever since about bringing them back and making permanent, loving homes for them...wishing we each had the room.

By the way, I have arranged for three spays, four neuters, gratis, at two of my vets...and they are supposed to come back here for surgery and convalescence. However, as Christine and I have shared with each other, this concerns us.

How will I possibly be able to send them off in another direction a second time? I am honestly agonizing over this. Christine and I, quite openly and possessively, consider the four of them to be "Our Four."

Jan Davidson

Last Leg for the Fab Four

As the Great Bunny Transport embarked on its final leg, I almost wished it didn't have to end – but that wouldn't be fair to the rabbits, who weren't meant to live out their lives in cages, carriers, or cars.

Modesto, California, to Roseville, California, 91 miles
Kim DeWoody, RW BGRR Conductor

Janet Foster and I met Jan and her son Ken in Modesto, California, on February 10, 2006, for the Fab Four's last leg of their trip. Rhett, Scarlett, Jackson, and Binkers all had the look of "Here we go again. People sticking their faces in front of me oohing and aahing."

On our return to Roseville, Janet and I had to do some fast rearranging of fostering plans. The foster home that they were to go to had to back out at the last minute. The Fab Four ended up staying a couple of days with Janet but are now in their permanent foster home until their forever homes come along.

Rhett, Scarlett, and Binkers were due for a trip back down to Fish Camp with Jan for a few weeks. She has received donated spay/neuter for them. Once again, we had to rearrange plans since Jan was snowed in by uncustomary spring storms.

In the meantime, they seem to be more relaxed every day. Their diet first just consisted of hay and pellets. When I started to introduce fresh veggies, their curious nature had them checking them out, but they didn't know what to do with them.

They are all quick learners, and while watching the other rabbits pig out, quickly figured out that the veggies were for eating and they were very good. They now wait just as impatiently as the other rabbits for their nightly salads!

Both Rhett and Scarlett have also discovered that being cuddled and petted feels very nice. Binkers, on the other hand, is still very cautious. It brought tears to my eyes the first time she came close enough to me to chin my finger.

She is quickly figuring out that a hand approaching her cage is a good thing. It brings the food and hay she enjoys so much. They all also enjoy kicking up their heels on the Bunny 500 and exploring the rabbit tunnel in the exercise area.

Our little Jackson has his own story. He came to us with an umbilical hernia and an old eye injury that, when it healed, caused some of the eyelashes to turn in, which irritated his cornea. He always seemed to have a scowl on his face. When you picked him up, he curled into a ball, reminding me of a little hedgehog. He never seemed to move *from his hunched position. You knew he had moved because his food was gone but he never let you see him do it.*

He has now been neutered, his hernia repaired, and had the offending eyelashes removed.

His tummy is white and fuzzy with the hair starting to grow back. Last night, he had his first butt bath. I've tried to wait as long as I could to give him any kind of bath so as not to stress him out any more than he already seemed to be, but he couldn't wait any longer.

He was a trooper! I think he actually seemed to enjoy it. He sat in my lap like a perfect gentleman while I gently rubbed him dry. I was just tickled when he started to get curious and stretched out to investigate things.

At dinner-time, after being put back into his cage, he came to the front instead of cowering in the back. This morning, he came to the front of the cage as if to say "Hi! What do you have good to eat?"

It's wonderful and very rewarding to watch the daily progress all of them are making! I wouldn't hesitate to do it all again!

Kim DeWoody
A New Hope Animal Foundation
Vice President & Rabbit Program Manager

I heard from Jennifer not long after the Katrina rabbits landed in California. She had spent a little over a month coordinating their transport and yet, she was already busy making arrangements for other rabbits to go home.

As we speak I am in the process of coordinating five transports:

- *Eight rabbits going from Silver Spring, Maryland, to Whittaker, Michigan*
- *One rabbit going from Appleton, Wisconsin, to Scranton, Pennsylvania (the forever home is in Connecticut)*

- *One rabbit going from New Orleans, Louisiana (Kemo), to Miami, Florida*
- *Two rabbits going from Virginia, to Boise, Idaho*
- *One rabbit (Louise who was transported by Jan/Ken) going from Fish Camp, California, to Renee in Houston, Texas*

Jennifer

The Katrina rabbits were survivors. Having lived through the greatest natural disaster of our time, they were now safely in foster care. This was cause for great celebration. The efforts of so many across so many miles had been worth it all. These bunnies were almost home.

Chapter Seven
FOSTER PARENTS

The foster home opens up their home to the dog, gives the dog a warm bed, a soft pillow, some good food, and a place to just chill until he or she heads on their way.

Lorraine Ehrhart
Miami-Dade Rescue Railroad

Debbie Fahrenholtz is no ordinary foster parent. She's a proud foster Mom to dogs, especially female dogs rescued from puppy mills. When I first met Debbie, I was taken with her gentleness. Her eyes were those of a woman who cared not only for small broken-down dogs, but for everything living.

As Debbie and I walked through her backyard play space accompanied by itty-bitty dogs, a tiny creature named Betty struggled to take a step without falling over. Her gallant efforts to move one foot forward at a time caused me to cringe.

Another rescued mill dog named Jazzy let me cuddle her very soft, fragile body in my arms. I gazed at Betty, the bruised and battered creature teetering on the ground.

Betty, the rescued puppy mill Yorkie.

Debbie's day-to-day life has been altered by the deeds of puppy millers and these teeny rescued dogs. She's still amazed at Betty's willingness to survive and forgive…

I got involved personally just by doing some searching on the internet one day trying to find a foster program to work with dogs and came across Puppy Mill Rescue, filled out an application, and just got very involved with being a foster Mom; and slowly got more and more involved with the group, and working with the dogs.

Betty was rescued from a breeder in Missouri. She was rescued through a humane society in Missouri. They pulled her and about thirty other dogs from this place, all Yorkies, in very, very bad condition.

They were covered with parasites, they were covered with lice, they had not eaten a good meal in a long time. Betty, being blind, we suspect was probably the least fed because it took her a long while to find the food bowls.

She also has no teeth, so it made it very difficult for her to eat — so she was very emaciated, very weak. She could not hold her head up once she was rescued. She had no muscle tone whatsoever, was mostly bald, most of her hair had fallen out from the lice and malnutrition.

I asked warily about the lives of puppy mill breeding dogs, almost knowing the news wouldn't be good.

Puppy mill dogs spend their lives in a cage. Their whole purpose for being is to make puppies and to make money for the puppy miller or commercial breeder.

Most of the time they live on wire bottom cages so their feet are constantly splayed by the wire and cut by the wire. They live in their own feces and urine. If they're lucky enough to be on the top tier of a puppy mill cage it falls through; if they're unlucky to live on the bottom, they get the stuff from the top.

They have very little if any vet care from the day that they're born, they are bred every heat cycle so their little bodies get used up really fast…A dog goes into heat twice a year so they work real hard on getting at least two litters of puppies from a mill dog every year.

They are untreated for injuries or diseases or illnesses, the ammonia that builds up in their cages from the urine and feces causes them to be blind, with ulcers on their eyes and their feet.

They have skin issues. They are never socialized with people. When they are handled, they're handled roughly and without much care. They never walk on grass, they never know what it's like to live in a house, to eat good food, to have fresh clean water all the time, to feel loved…

Betty's strained gait and withered frame tells me she has experienced all of the above. How on earth do mill dogs ever get out of those situations?

We get some of them through auctions in the Midwest where dogs are sold. A lot of times we get them through humane societies or police departments or shelter workers who go in and close a place down because it's not up to standards, so we occasionally get them that way.

Also, we get them through vets, when vets get them turned over to them for euthanasia or disposal. We actually sometimes get them from the breeders themselves. A lot of them deal directly with rescue groups.

Sometimes we go undercover and get them that way, either by going into the mills and buying them, or posing as breeders ourselves, or even posing as people looking for pets and wanting an older dog, maybe not a puppy to start with.

Once they've been rescued, puppy mill dogs are transported to their new lives, sometimes thousands of miles away.

We have a lot of different ways that we use to transport dogs, most of them with volunteers. One of those that Puppy Mill Rescue is involved with and actually started five years ago is a group called Truck-N-Paws.

We have lots of volunteers that work relaying dogs across the country and relaying them to either foster homes or permanent homes.

I wondered if Debbie found it hard to walk away from puppies on display in pet store windows. She held Betty close, and ever so carefully. Her heartfelt reply stung like a bee.

When you do go into the pet store and you see that puppy and you can't resist and you buy it, this is the mother that's left behind in a cage a thousand miles away making more and more puppies over and over again until she's all used up, and broken and hurting. Betty suffers for what you buy in the pet stores. The pain and hurt that she goes through for those puppies is just not worth it.

Just when I thought Debbie was finished, she wasn't.

The puppy mill industry and the commercial breeding industry are driven by what drives most of us — money. We're all out to make a living…Unfortunately, a lot of what people do to do that doesn't take into account the other beings that we share this planet with.

Just because we walk upright and have thumbs doesn't mean that we are more deserving of respect and a happy, healthy, cared for life than a dog or a cow or a camel.

Debbie Fahrenholtz
Puppy Mill Rescue Foster Mom

I saw Debbie again a month later. She showed me a beautiful stone bearing the likeness of her beloved dog Pepper, which had been cast for her by a friend. It was as if she knew I was awash in the sadness of slowly losing our dear Husky boy, who looked just like Pepper! The stone's image was too much for me, and I lost my professional demeanor and cried.

Debbie kindly sought to provide comfort but my consolation actually came from Betty, who looked much improved. I borrowed some courage from the brave little Yorkie girl and drove away.

We lost Nika soon afterward. He is still very much missed, though his soft silver and white Husky hair no longer lingers in every corner of our home.

◆◆◆

My search for a breed-specific foster home took me back to New Hampshire. It was close to Christmas and as usual for these northerly parts, it was freezing cold. If anything could take the chill out of a New England winter afternoon, it would be an assembly of leaping Dachshunds gathered at the door.

Stepping inside, I was invited into a warmly decorated room. Colorful dog toys, stockpiles of chewies, little blankets, and comfy beds were scattered about. Adjacent was a closet full of designer duds for the little dogs to wear. I decided then and there that if I were a homeless Dachshund, this is where I'd want to be, here in Dachshund Heaven with Sandy Clabaugh.

I knew that this foster Mom, who was also a veteran transport coordinator, specialized in caring for special needs dogs. What an unselfish soul, I thought, watching three small dogs with middles shaped like hot dogs vie for her attention.

Sandy set the record straight as she reached for a black and tan puppy whose diapered derriere wiggled when he walked.

I get my greatest satisfaction from caring for special needs dogs. I love my healthy ones, I love all of them, but there is something very special about a special needs dog.

I tell everybody that there is nothing self-less about what I do. I am very selfish, and I get all of the rewards from taking care of them.

The pup Sandy named Miles was an absolute charmer. In retrospect, his charm may have spared his life.

Miles was born in Virginia. We know that the breeder had about fifty dogs, (so basically, a puppy mill) and he was sold to a woman. She got him for a reduced price, and

Puppy Miles.

*it wasn't until she got him home that she realized he didn't
have bowel or bladder control, so she took him to her vet.*

The Virginia vet's diagnosis was that he probably had ectopic ureters. This meant that the tiny pipelines that carry urine from the kidneys to the bladder weren't connected to his bladder, which was most likely the cause of the constant leakage. Add to that a prolapsed rectum and a possible disc missing in his spine....

I held onto my very weak stomach as Sandy grabbed for tissues and casually cleaned up after Miles. Why was this impish Dachshund born this way?

Whatever the source of his troubles, Sandy was dealing with the consequences, which earned her the right to vent.

> *The people who are breeding the dogs for money rather
> than for the quality of the dogs are not paying attention
> to genetics. They're simply [saying] "Here's a Cocker and
> here's a Cocker and let's put them together and have some
> Cocker puppies."*
>
> *With Dachshunds we find that "Oh, here's a Dapple
> Dachshund and here's a Dapple Dachshund and let's put
> them together" without realizing Double-Dap puppies are
> going to be blind and deaf. The other thing that we see
> are behavior issues, because there's a lot of inbreeding going*

on within the mills, and there's also a tremendous lack of socialization for the puppies.

You've got fifty dogs in crates, and feces dripping through them and the puppies aren't getting the proper care, and they're grabbed from their Moms at five weeks and they're thrown into another crate.... Then they're stuck in another crate and put on a truck and moved, and then another crate in a pet store, and then people wonder why when they're four months old they're biting!

They have some tremendous baggage that they're carrying because of the situation with bad breeders.

Miles looked up at Sandy as if to remind her to continue his story, and she gave him a little kiss.

So it was really looking bad for this boy. One of the members of my rescue group worked at the vet's and had seen him, thought he was pretty adorable, and asked if anyone on the list was willing to give him a chance or do anything with him.

I called my vet and told her what these vets had said, and she said, "Sandy, it wouldn't be wrong to put him down," and I said "Well, but would it be wrong to not put him down?"

So I told the member that I would take him. I have a wonderful neurologist, and I knew that he would be able to take a look at him and tell me something.

A volunteer transporter had a hand in getting Miles to New Hampshire.

There was a woman that helped move Miles when he came up from Virginia and I still hear from her, and she just was so impressed with Miles as a puppy and so happy to be a part of that rescue. She played a role in saving a dog, and being a transport driver plays a role.

What we found out when Dr. Potthoff saw him was that the tail was not connected to the spine.

Sandy was surprised when a bare-bottomed puppy was returned to her after surgery. Miles did not have ectopic ureters or discs missing in his spine after all. His troubles were neurological, and his deformed tail had been getting in the way.

He started acupuncture, and we got a diet developed for him, and through all of this he has come a long, long way. He's never going to have bowel or bladder control, or at least not totally. The bellybands are great, the pants are great, and I've just kind of learned to live with it I guess, which is the secret to it all.

Like any foster pup, Sandy knew Miles deserved a permanent home. The jazzy-diaper clad Dachshund was put up for adoption.

He was on the website for six months and during that period I had a couple of people who were interested in adopting him. One wanted to keep him in their kitchen all the time.

Well, he had been living here with all the others with pads strung on everything so he wouldn't make a mess, but he was one of the other dogs. I didn't want him living separated from other dogs.

Another person interested in him said "Well, most of the time he would be with the other dogs, except when the other dogs went into the rooms with carpet."

Well again, I didn't want him differentiated and I had some concerns. Would he be able to go on trips with them?

So I kind of got strict on, "These are the requirements; you have to treat him like you do your other dogs," and I'm sure I restricted the number of people who applied for him, but he was just too normal a dog to not be able to have a normal environment.

Miles licked Sandy's face as if he agreed that yes, he preferred to be treated like a normal dog.

And then after about six months I got an inquiry that looked really good. I thought for sure that this was going to be the right one, and I have to say when I read the inquiry my heart dropped to my feet. I wrote her back, and every time I would open my email, my heart was in my throat. Is there going to be an application? Is there going to be another email? When is she going to want to meet him? What are we going to do? And every day I became more and more convinced that I just did not want to give him up.

Sandy dramatically gestured through the recounting of her emotional tug-of-war.

And so it became a debate: here's all the really good reasons I should give him up, and the only thing over here was but I really, really love him.

So all these rational reasons, and this one reason of the heart, and I decided that no, he belonged here. He is now officially adopted. He has "adopted" listed by him on the website. He has a home, and he's staying here forever.

Though not everyone who fosters gravitates toward special needs, Sandy hoped individuals would consider a few things before signing up for duty.

Happy Miles.

First of all you have to love them. The next thing is, I think you have to be prepared for problems, and you have to know something about the breed. This applies to anybody, whether they're talking about Dachshunds or Dobermans or Rotties.

You need to understand the breed because you're going to see a little bit of everything that breed can present, and the first thing to do is to figure out if you're one of those people.

Do you have the time, do you have the energy, do you have other dogs in your home who are going to accept that? Are you able to say good-bye after they've been there for a while?

Sandy Clabaugh
Almost Home Dachshund Rescue

Miles yawned and settled into one of his heart-stealing poses. Looking around at the other contented and impeccably cared for dogs, I shook my head. My time with them had been short, yet they had my heart wrapped around theirs from the moment the door opened. I knelt down and said good-bye to Miles, Blossom, Thumper, Mouse, and Toby the blind Cocker.

No, it wasn't realistic, but I left hoping Sandy would eventually adopt them all.

Chapter Eight
FOREVER HOMES

A "forever home," we were told by people in the business of helping animals get there, is that special place where an animal will be loved, wanted, and cared for – for the rest of his or her life.

It wasn't long after we interviewed Debbie that she announced the perfect forever home had been found for Betty. The blind little Yorkie girl whose courage had so inspired us would soon become Grandma to a delegation of adoring Chihuahuas. She would be forever loved, wanted, and cared for by two canine-smitten women in Pennsylvania.

> *After losing our two precious babies (Chihuahuas), we searched online in hopes of finding another dog to help fill the void. It was then that we discovered Puppy Mill Rescue.*
>
> *After reading only a few paragraphs, we were so disgusted and so enraged we had to learn more about these puppy mills. We thoroughly researched their website and also discovered two little Chi's that we knew were meant for us.*
>
> *So we applied and were granted permission to adopt those two babies – rescued from a mill. Within a month we adopted three more mill dogs. It hadn't taken us very long to see how damaged some of these dogs were and how very different they were from our last two Chi's, that had passed away.*
>
> *We became even more involved with PMR and with a local group trying to shut down these horrible mills. Since*

we live right next to the "puppy mill capital," Lancaster, PA, we have our work cut out for us.

We soon learned about Ms. Betty and we were lucky enough to meet her in June 2005 at a Dog Walk held in Lancaster County. Her foster Mom, Debbie Fahrenholtz, brought her down from Rhode Island to attend the dog walk.

It was love at first sight. Her determination to live after all she'd been through was so intriguing to us. We knew we had all the love this girl deserved and she belonged with us.

Once approved to adopt Betty, her foster Mom, Debbie, made arrangements so that she could deliver our new addition directly to us. So on August 10, 2005, she arrived.

Since we are only about six to seven hours from Debbie, and she needed to do our home inspection, we decided not to use Truck-N-Paws and Debbie brought Ms. Betty right to us.

Surprisingly, Betty seemed to adjust quite well in her new home. Considering she is blind and deaf, consistency in her surroundings is very important. But she adapted very quickly to our home. It took us longer to get used to her than for her to us.

We were so worried for her and about her all the time. We were afraid she'd run into things and be scared because she wouldn't "recognize" anything. Well, she did bump into everything but we learned that that's how she'll get familiar with our home – trial and error.

She didn't seem fazed by it at all. She took it all in stride. At the time, we had five other dogs, all Chi's, so she was the "odd man out." She didn't seem to mind them at all, but the Chi's seemed reluctant to get near her.

Whenever she would bump into them, they would be disturbed, as if to say, "Yo...didn't you see me laying here?"

I think it took the Chi's a while to learn that the bumping into them and other things was just the way it was.

I think they learned pretty quickly that Betty was different from them – and not just because she was a Yorkie. They sensed her disabilities and none of them were ever mean to her. She was revered.

Today we have nine dogs (one of them is a foster) and they all do very well with each other. Betty has become a part of the gang. We often find one or more of the other dogs laying with Betty in her bed, and I think Betty enjoys the company.

She wakes up around 5:00 am each day. She wiggles herself up onto her feet, her diaper falls off, and she begins her morning walk (in circles) through the living room/dining room. By this time one of

Ms. Betty in bed…and doing her business.

us is up and she is carried out to the yard to do her business with the other dogs.

Once back inside, she begins her frantic search for breakfast. I don't think her sense of smell is all too good. So we quickly prepare her blended dog food with water to a smooth consistency, since she has no teeth.

She's taken into a separate room to eat so she can have the entire bowl of food all to herself, without anyone else stealing any. It takes her a while to eat – she bobs her head into the bowl – I guess that's the way she learned to eat without teeth.

She often gets lost from the dish and after several circles around the room, she finds the dish again. If we happen to see her straying from the bowl, we help her back to the dish. This is why it takes her so long to eat.

After breakfast she has the dreaded face washing. We must wash her face after each meal since there is food clear up to her forehead and often on the tops of each ear. She's given her eye ointment, for dry eyes, twice a day. Then she's diapered and ready to relax on her bed.

She sleeps most of the day. Her hungry belly wakes her up when it's dinner time. And the routine starts over again. The other dogs go about their business – playing, running, barking – but Betty just lays in her bed and rests.

She has no idea what "playing" is. We've never heard her bark, either. With the warmer weather arriving, Betty actually loves the outdoors. We take her out along with the other eight. When we go to check on them five minutes later, she is clear down to the end of the yard – all the other dogs are waiting to come back in.

Somehow she has made her way down from one end of the yard to the other. She usually travels in circles – I guess this helps her "feel" her way. She really likes being out in the sun, although we have to be mindful of her getting a sunburn, due to her very thin hair. I believe she can see some light – so when the sun is shining on her, she loves it.

I think Betty made up her mind a long time ago that no matter what life she is dealt, she's going to face it head on and make the most of it. Aside from her eye meds, she isn't on any other medications. She has gained some weight since her release from the mill. She could stand to gain a little more, but she's gotten a clean bill of health from the vet.

She still has a hernia that was never treated while in the mill, but apparently doesn't need to be treated now, the risk of being under anesthesia is too great. She just turned sixteen years old, so surgery is not advisable.

I think any puppy mill dog IS a special needs dog. You need to accept caring for a PM dog with an open mind. You need to have a lot of patience. It is very rewarding, too.

It's the most exciting thing to see these dogs become "real" dogs. We kind of refer to it as the Pinocchio-effect. When they first come out of the mills, they are scared stiff. When attempting to pick them up, they slink to the ground and become dead weight. They have no idea what to do with people.

*But slowly, after a lot of one-on-one work with these dogs, they start to trust, they start to let their guards down, they actually start coming **to** people for petting and attention – they start to become "real." They realize people aren't all that bad.*

Before we saw her, we wanted her. Before we met her, we loved her. Before she was here one hour, we would die for her. She captured our hearts.

Cindy Myers and Deb Haney
Pennsylvania

Not every dog is as fortunate as Betty to be adopted into a nearby state. The ride to a forever home would be much longer for a cruelty case named Buck. The twenty-one volunteers who delicately knit themselves together to aid a permanently disfigured dog were all strangers to this young, friendly canine. All except for one.

Buck is just so special…I always said he has an angel on his shoulder because he has escaped death so many times.

Deanna Trietsch, Volunteer

The innocent pup's troubles began at a very early age. An Officer with the Rutherford County Animal Control facility in Murfreesboro, Tennessee, took the call that saved Buck's life, at least for the first time.

I received a call about the animal abuse apparently from someone who knew the owner and may have even been there when it occurred. When I got to the owner's home he was not there, so I left him a warning to contact us.

He did contact us the next day, and I asked him about the dogs. He stated that he had cut the male's ears with a pair of scissors and had a rubber band around his tail to get it to fall off. He stated that he had used some kind of pain medication but could not produce it.

I confiscated the male pup, who was about eight weeks old, and ordered him to bring the female to the shelter. (I think his wife had the female at the time.) He brought the

  *female in and was arrested while at the shelter by MPD.*

Buck —a cruelty case with a happy ending.

I took both k9s to one of the veterinarians I know and that helps us when she can. The k9s were treated. I think she kept them for a few days.

We won the case in court for animal cruelty. He did not get any jail time for the animal cruelty charge, but he was already facing about eighteen years on probation. He ended up, as far as I know, going back to jail for a while. His wife was convicted as well.

Johnny J. Crivello
Animal Control Officer

Dr. Carmen Stallman treated Buck. She confronted Buck's owner about the state of Buck's ears and tail.

He said that it had been too expensive to get the ear crop done, so he had just "sawed" them off with scissors. I told him that was inhumane, and "How would he like it if someone did that to him?"

He then changed his story and said he got anesthetic – I asked where, and then he changed it to using ace – which is a tranquilizer and not a pain med.

When I described the state of infection and how bad the ears looked, he then asked if I could fix the ears to make them look better. He had no concern for the dog.

Buck was kept at our clinic for several months. We amputated the tail correctly as the end was dead but not separated from the base, and kept him on antibiotics for the ears.

It is hard to imagine how he felt as his ears were, as the owner put it, sawed through with scissors at ten weeks of age.

Dr. Carmen Stallman

After he had recovered (at least physically) from his terrible ordeal, Buck was brought to a local shelter, where his pitiful appearance stole the heart of a volunteer.

One day I was donating some pet carriers to the Rutherford County Animal Control facility in Murfreesboro, Tennessee, and while there just decided to go in the adoption room and visit the fur-orphans.

In the first row of kennels at the very end there was a dog that took my breath away...that dog was Buck. He stood out because he was an obvious case of severe cruelty – having had the tops of his ears brutally cut off...

It's the first time I'd seen anything like that...but despite his past history this dog was as sweet as pie, very friendly and wanted nothing more than to get out of the shelter and into a loving home.

I left the shelter but Buck did not leave my mind... I was absolutely haunted by him and could not forget his face. I can still, to this day, see him as clear as day how he looked at me and with those ears of his chopped off.

A couple weeks passed and I knew his time was running out at the shelter, which at the time had about a 95-98 percent euthanasia rate....

In fact, the only reason Buck wasn't put to sleep was the fact that he was a cruelty case that had touched the hearts of the shelter workers!

Anyhow, I called back to see if Buck was still there or if he'd been put to sleep. Happily the shelter told me that Buck had been adopted!

I was ecstatic and could now get some sleep! My happiness was short-lived, however, because on my next visit to the same shelter, guess who was there once again behind bars – none other than Buck! Bless his heart.

Evidently the woman who adopted him made some very lame excuse as to why she couldn't keep him, and he was now again in danger of being euthanized. This time, the shelter would not be able to keep him as long. Once again, I'm haunted by Buck.

Deanna Trietsch, volunteer

Deanna wasn't the only person who would be haunted by Buck. Many hundreds of miles away in Phoenix, Arizona, Holly Thomas was at her computer, trying to find help for an emaciated stray running around her neighborhood. She came across Buck's shelter photos and the plea for someone to adopt him.

Meet Buck. He's 7 1/2 months old.
Very friendly. Had a difficult life so far.
He's already neutered. $26 springs him from the shelter.
That covers parvo/distemper, rabies, and initial worming.
Hope you can help him out. Poor guy could be a
poster dog for animal abuse!
Thanks,
Peggy
Rutherford Co. Animal Services/volunteer
1140 Haley Road
Murfreesboro, TN 37130

Personally, I could not walk away from my computer after seeing his sad eyes. I could not sleep the weekend after seeing his plea to be adopted circulating the internet. Buck did nothing wrong, and deserved a chance at a full and happy life.

Holly Thomas

Buck's picture haunted Holly until the adoption approval process, which was all handled by phone, fax, and email, was finished. Though he now had a family waiting to offer him a forever home in Arizona, Buck was still an out-of-time dog. He would need to leave Rutherford County's Animal Control facility quickly due to space limitations.

A rescuer pulled Buck out of the shelter for Holly and took him to a home in Knoxville, Tennessee, where he was fostered for a few weeks. Buck went on to another foster home in Milan, Tennessee, for three more weeks. Both of these foster homes were arranged by Hearts of Gold Pit Bull Rescue in Memphis and served as a safe haven for Buck until transport could be arranged. During this time Holly recalls:

It was very stressful as to how we would actually move Buck from Tennessee to Phoenix until Elizabeth's transport request came through for Paddy, another dog being transported from Tennessee. I looked into having Buck flown but the temp in Arizona is too hot, and he would have had to go to Los Angeles. I looked into paying a private firm, however he would have been on a "caravan" for three weeks.

Holly Thomas

Buck's transport was coordinated and moderated by Dr. Elizabeth C. Sescilla, President and Founder of N.C.A.R.E.S, North Carolina Animal Resource & Education Services.

When I heard that he was in danger of being killed in a shelter and there was a great home waiting for him, I knew that a little effort on my part and on the part of some drivers for one weekend could buy Buck an entire lifetime.

How could I say no when mileage was the only thing standing between life and death for a dog who had been through so much in his short life? I couldn't.

Dr. Elizabeth C. Sescilla

The transport came down to the last three legs (Grants, New Mexico, to Flagstaff, Arizona) not being filled. Interstate 40 is a hard area to fill transports.

After waiting over a month to finally get Buck, we were not going to let the efforts of so many fall short and let the transport fall apart, so we made the commitment of driving round trip to Grants from Phoenix to meet Buck and Paddy.

Holly Thomas

While Holly and her husband, David were engrossed in preparations to charter three arduous desert legs, someone else was getting ready to meet the transport many miles east.

In the meantime, I had volunteered to drive on a transport where an LA Times Reporter and photographer would be coming along to do a story on a dog called Paddy, and perhaps a second fur-passenger needing to hitch a ride to their forever home would be joining up on this transport going out West.

I met the transport for Paddy in Nashville driving to hook up with the other driver who would have this "other dog" that was supposed to join the transport going west to Arizona then on to California.

Got to the meeting destination and lo-and-behold guess what dog popped out of that red truck that the other driver was in? It was Buck! The same cruelty case dog I'd seen at the Murfreesboro, Tennessee, high kill-shelter!

*I couldn't believe my eyes. The chances of me seeing a dog on death row in a shelter and then driving on a transport for that very same dog is nothing short of **divine intervention**. I could have fainted right there on the spot.*

It was probably one of the happiest moments of my life – to know that this dog that had haunted me with worry for so many weeks would be on one of my transports heading to a forever home was simply unforgettable. I knew in that very moment that God truly does care for His creatures great and small.

Deanna Trietsch

Planning and coordinating dog transports is never easy, but always rewarding. This trip was a long one that not only required people willing to drive for a few hours, but also two overnight stays along the route.

It's never easy to coordinate that many people over such a long distance, but because everyone who volunteers for a task such as this is motivated by compassion, it is not impossible.

Whether there are road detours, unexpected emergencies, etc., when you're dealing with a group of people with such character and compassion, you know you can count on them to come through no matter the obstacle.

Dr. Elizabeth C. Sescilla

Both David (my husband) and I were extremely excited and anxious waiting to see Buck. We received updates from Elizabeth as well as each person that handled Buck and Paddy for each leg of their transport from Tennessee to Grants, New Mexico.

When David and I met Amy (one of the transport drivers) in Grants, both Buck and Paddy were waiting in a little gravel area for us. Buck was skittish about getting back into a car, but once settled in he did fine.

There were twenty-one people who volunteered their homes, cars, gas money, and their time to transport or overnight Buck on his journey.

Without these volunteers, our Transport Coordinator, drivers, and overnights, we would not have been able to move Buck from Milan, Tennessee (foster home #2) to Phoenix, Arizona.

Even after the stress of trying to figure out how to get him from Point A to Point B, all the effort by everyone was worth it and very much appreciated.

Holly Thomas

Buck is Blessed

Buck has totally changed our lives. He makes us laugh and gives us comfort when he knows we are upset or not feeling well. He senses when things are not one hundred percent and gives us his paw, like he is trying to tell us it will be okay. He is a total cuddle muffin and loves to snuggle as close as he can to the pillows.

He loves to go to the dog park and be chased by the other dogs. He loves going for rides in the car and taking walks around our neighborhood.

Buck running at the dog park.

People that see Buck look at David and me like we are the ones that cut his ears. We are both adamant about telling Buck's story – how we rescued him, and that he was a cruelty seizure case.

One lady at a Blessing of the Pets stopped me and asked what happened to his ears. I told her Buck's story and her response was "Have you thought of cosmetic sur-

gery?" I couldn't believe it. I advised her that he's been through enough and he survived, and I would never alter his appearance now.

It was heartbreaking to finally find out the true story behind his abuse. My husband and I are amazed at what Buck suffered at such an early age, and what an amazing personality he has considering the abuse.

We truly believe that Buck is happy and content with our family. He has the biggest smile and happiest wiggly butt that you will ever see.

Holly Thomas

Buck at his forever home.

Chapter Nine
VOLUNTEERS

*We transport about twenty-five to twenty-eight dogs
every weekend. Transport is one of the most important ingredients in rescue. And the volunteers are golden, priceless if you may. They are the key to any rescue's success. If
we did not have volunteers bringing the dogs to adoptions,
no one would see them to adopt them.*

Rande Levine
Karma Rescue

I had just hung up the phone after talking with Kim, who
manages the volunteers at the Rutherford County shelter. She too
described her volunteer staff as a priceless group of people who
show up faithfully to comfort animals, post their pictures, and
assist with adoptions.

I thought about the incredible number of volunteers who had a
part in getting Buck from Tennessee to Arizona.

Kim remembered Buck well, and told me that although she now
works at a sparkling new facility, Buck had lived at the old dimly
lit, poorly designed one. He and the other dogs were held in grim
kennels with slatted flooring that Kim considered inhumane. She re-
called Buck's toes getting caught over and over in between the slats
until they turned red and became swollen. Kim was thrilled to hear
of Buck's good fortune and his forever home. She explained why her
shelter needs volunteers now more than ever.

The Murfreesboro area is experiencing an incredible growth
spurt. Large farms are being purchased by developers and subdivided

into much smaller land slices for single-family homes.

Many of the new residents arrive from outside the area, often times with animal ethics that are different from some of the long-time residents. This has resulted in a greater number of calls to Animal Control from people who are appalled to see so many strays, unleashed bully breed dogs, and animals left tied outdoors in all kinds of weather with no source of shelter.

Kim and her volunteers work hard taking care of a never-ending stream of animal emergencies, but manage to spend time talking with people about how they can make life better for animals in their corner of Tennessee. She shared with me that one of the toughest obstacles she and her volunteers face is not ignorance, but arrogance, because when arrogance is present, there is no room for discussion nor possibility for change. There is only a stubborn unwillingness to do things any other way than the way things have always been done.

I wasn't sure how people who work helping animals counteract something like arrogance. And how do volunteers like Lorraine keep up the frenzied pace, the cheerleading, and the diplomacy required to spring animals from their dire circumstances, every single week?

> To continue in animal rescue takes an incredible amount of commitment, an incredible amount of stamina, because they just keep coming.

> Every week it's another fifty, sixty dogs, animals that you're looking at and you think okay, whew, we got them out, and then it just is staggering, it never, ever stops.

> We would love to see Miami-Dade Rescue Railroad be able to service so many more animals and so many more rescue groups but that takes resources....

> It takes money and it takes volunteers, and this business is a high burn-out business because it's so emotional, so sometimes you can't keep a volunteer active for a very long period of time. So that makes the need for volunteers even all the more greater.

This pitiful pup was brought into the shelter as a stray just before Christmas. One of our wonderful foster moms, Barbara Arco, volunteered to foster her. She said that the experience was to be her Christmas present to herself.

Noelle before...

Lorraine Ehrhart, Director
Miami-Dade Rescue Railroad

As Christmas approached, and just a day after a very young pup died of Parvo while in my care for only a few hours, I opened an e-mailed photo of a pathetically skinny, scared, scaly, and hairless puppy that had only a few days left at the pound – if she made it that long.

Knowing that time was essential, and notwithstanding my self-doubt and guilt over the Parvo pup, I volunteered to foster and care for the puppy that was still, albeit barely, alive. Little did I know then that the experience would turn into one of the proudest and joyous of my life. The puppy was aptly named Noelle.

When I first saw Noelle, she was grossly undernourished, frail, and fearful. Instead of hair, her raw, reddened skin was covered with scabs and lesions. Used to being shunned, insulted, abused, and neglected, she cowered in the backseat of the transport car.

It took so little – a kind word, a soft, caring touch, a welcome lap – to expose her pure heart, soulful eyes and irrepressible spirit. But the fight that she and I, and the wonderful network of people who helped and would help, faced had just begun.

No one but Noelle, and those responsible for her horrific condition, knows how she came to be abandoned and *so debilitated. Her most serious affliction was generalized (meaning all over her body) Demodectic mange, which is not contagious, but is more difficult to treat and cure than Sarcoptic mange (scabies).*

Ironically, stress triggers an outbreak if a dog is prone to demodicosis. This nasty condition caused her such misery – constantly itching skin with large pustules cov-

ering her body that would spontaneously burst and ooze pus and blood.

As if that wasn't enough to endure, the mange severely compromised her immune system, allowing other diseases, most significantly upper and lower respiratory infections, to

Noelle during…

infiltrate.

Treatment required a systemic approach to combat the systemic nature of her condition. But her weak little body couldn't take it. Until the right medical protocol was designed, I nearly lost Noelle at least three times during the first two weeks.

Each time, she fought back the fevers, congestion, and intestinal attacks. She was too weak to walk or stand. Nevertheless, she didn't mess her bedding, but cooperated when I carried her outside where she relieved herself while maintaining her innate sense of pride. She tolerated everything, including multiple stomach-upsetting antibiotics, twice-daily nebulizer treatments, and more.

Every time we thought she was out of the woods, she plunged closer to death. But she never gave up. Because of that, no one else did either.

The e-mails and calls flooded in with suggestions, prayers, and encouragement. Caring persons, most notably "Auntie Sue," visited to cheer her (and me) and to lend a hand. The outpouring from the rescue network and friends was overwhelming. It emboldened me and gave me the strength to keep fighting.

In turn, Noelle fed off of the strength and rallied. By New Year's Day, Noelle was breathing without difficulty, taking short walks (something totally new to her), and playing! It was my most cherished gift of the season.

On her recent visit to Aardvark Animal Hospital, which is heaven on earth for the most helpless and hopeless, Noelle was declared "mite-free." If she remains so for two more weeks, Dr. Fernandes said he will release her from further care.

At that time, she will be available for adoption to a lucky forever family. Although letting her go will be the hardest and saddest thing I will have to do, I am comforted by knowing it is best for her.

Noelle deserves to be the center of attention in a good and loving home, perhaps with children as happy and full of life as she is, and to enjoy a life that makes up for everything that she has been through. She has given

...and Noelle after treatment.

me so much – pride and joy, cherished memories, connections with people I would never have had – it is the least that I can give to her.

Barbara Arco
Volunteer

Every animal that you pull out of that shelter is so special...they all look at you the same way, and that's with such gratitude. They know, whether it's a puppy or an old Shih Tzu, you can see the gratitude in their eyes...

Lorraine Ehrhart
Miami-Dade Rescue Railroad

Chapter Ten

WALKER'S JOURNEY HOME

It was late October. We had accumulated lots of footage including some mini DV tapes sent to us by animal-loving producers in other parts of the country. One of the producers, Jennifer Warner in Santa Monica, introduced us to what we call the "California Tether."

Devised to keep dogs from jumping around in vehicles, the pre-doggie seat belt system requires that a knot be put in the dog's leash before it is tucked through the window and closed in the car door. A dog tethered in this manner can't do much more than sit on the car seat while in transit. According to the drivers who employ it, a short-leashed animal is indeed a calm passenger.

I didn't think this method of restraining dogs in vehicles would fly in Massachusetts, because everyone who sat beside me and watched the footage said it looked like the dogs were being hung. "And what if they got into an accident?" chimed our viewers almost on cue.

That's part of what made all of this so interesting. Transporters in different regions of the country seemed to have their own special way of getting animals to where they needed to go. If officials in Massachusetts had their way, I was told, rescued animals would no longer arrive via the volunteer animal transport network. The animals would be barred from entering the state.

"That's ridiculous," I said lightheartedly to a dog rescuer on the phone. "You mean if our family wanted to adopt a dog from Miami's Animal Services or Janet's rescue in North Carolina, we couldn't?"

"That's right," she replied. "Not under the new Emergency Order." "Emergency Order?" I repeated skeptically. Even the title rang like something from the old Soviet Union.

This obviously professional woman who was also well versed in Department of Agriculture law regarding the importation of dogs from other states continued, and her news shocked me.

Rescues in my freezing-cold-six-months-of-the-year state were being issued cease and desist orders, and officials were harassing and intimidating transporters, even if they were only passing through. Even worse, I was informed that dogs, including fully vetted puppies en route to New England destinations from other states, were being confiscated at the border, and sometimes handed over to kill-shelters.

Like any producer working on a documentary about volunteer animal transport would be, I was curious as to what in the world was going on. I called the authors of this great decree set forth without public input or comment at the Massachusetts Department of Agricultural Resources, and politely requested an interview. My calls were not returned.

Being a long-time resident of the state, I was duly insulted. If a small group of appointed decision makers were going to try to tell Bay Staters we couldn't adopt dogs from other states, the least they could do is tell us why.

I got a copy of the document and read it for myself. If someone had asked my opinion on the hurriedly drafted piece of writing, I would have said that the language contained therein was crass, condescending, threatening, and all about control.

Some transporters told me that if I wanted to know the true origin of the "Emergency Order," I should follow the money trail.

Pet storeowners and breeders had complained that too many rescued dogs were being adopted into the state, and would, they believed, eventually destroy their customer base. The Order could effectively clamp down on the influx of rescued animals, especially Southern rescued dogs, thereby limiting the financial losses of animal sellers. Proponents for the legislation claimed that the Order had nothing to do with selling animals for profit; it was created to address serious issues like keeping contagious diseases from infecting animals already registered and living in the great state of Massachusetts.

If Russ had been in the room with me then, he would have heard me deliver my longest "hmmmmm" ever.

A few animal lovers urged me to shift my focus and do an exposé on this whole "No animal immigrants allowed" thing occurring right here in my home state. I explained that I was no investigative reporter. That sort of producing requires a different skill set than I had, and besides, I loathed controversy and avoided it whenever possible. The seventies produced more lovers than fighters, and I was one of them. I was determined to stay focused, despite the chaos that had erupted for volunteers transporting animals to or through Massachusetts.

Frightfully concerned that the certified healthy animals in their care may be confiscated, the transporters reacted accordingly and their railroads went underground.

The run sheets posted on-line, which were normally filled with all kinds of vehicle and personal information meant to help transporters recognize one another, were being used, I was told, to aid Massachusetts officials in enforcing their new regulations.

The transporters decided to temporarily return, at least until someone threw tea overboard in Boston Harbor again, to the old-fashioned way of doing things. The on-line message boards still posted run sheets with dogs traveling south to north, but when the transport crossed over into Massachusetts, the information disappeared without a trace.

And so it was amidst this backdrop of suspicion, confusion, and fear that we decided to tape a Southern rescued dog en route to his forever home in New England.

◆◆◆

Walker's fifteen leg journey to his forever home was to be the public's first look at volunteer animal transport in action. The little Aussie-mix's long pilgrimage to an expectant, loving family would serve as our centerpiece, the crown jewel of our production. Most importantly, it would showcase one animal's triumph over what had befallen him as a puppy, and would demonstrate how people, by offering only an hour or so of their time, could help spare the life of a dog.

A poster distributed to veterinarians' offices, doggie day-care facilities, and a few other places in New Hampshire had resulted in several calls from people interested in adopting Walker.

PLEASE!

CAN YOU GIVE ME A HOME?

I am a very handsome 8-month-old Aussie-mix named Walker. I was rescued from a pound in North Carolina and have a free ride to New Hampshire via the volunteer animal transport network. I weigh only 40 lbs. and love children! Might you have room in your home (and heart) for me?

My name is Checkers. I am a 14-month-old Lab/Border Collie mix and weigh 85 lbs. I was rescued from a North Carolina pound. I am very loving, but I stand less of a chance of being adopted because I'm a big boy. I could take a free ride north with my friend Walker if someone will offer me a home.

If you would like to offer Walker or Checkers a home, please call 4 Paws Animal Rescue (704) 489-1251. Adoption donation greatly appreciated, as all vet work (including neuter) is complete and up to date!

Thank you for caring enough to inquire about these precious Dixie-land dogs...

Janet decided on a family who had fallen in love with Walker's photo. The Squatritos had three animal-loving children, plenty of space for Walker to run, and he would have a canine girlfriend, another Aussie named Chelsea. It was determined that once the adoption approval process was complete, Terri Epp would be asked if she could coordinate and monitor Walker's trip north.

My elaborate producer plans were churning. If Terri would allow it, we could include cameras at every hand-off, at the overnight Bed and Biscuit, and in each transport vehicle along the way.

Russ wanted to go one step further. He hoped to tape drivers at their homes getting ready to meet the other transporters, reality-style of course. The only way we could pull this off was for Terri to inform her drivers in advance and get everyone's approval.

I watched as Terri posted Walker's run sheet on the message boards. She began posting on Monday, October 31, just four days before the transport would need to hit the road. Brandy Holleran's OTRA (On The Road Again) posted Terri's request to the group's members.

```
[OnTheRoadAgain]
Transport Coordinator: Terri Epp
(terrilepp@yahoo.ca)
Transport Date: November 4-6, 2005
Denver, NC to Londonderry, NH
```

4 Paws Animal Rescue
6102 Sandal Creek Lane, Denver, NC
Contact: Janet Northrop (704) 489-1251
Email: fourpawsnc@yahoo.com
Website: http://www.fourpawsnc.petfinder.com

```
Name - Walker
Breed - Aussie mix
Age - 8 months
Sex - male, altered
Size - 40 lbs.
Up to date on immunizations, etc. - yes, trav-
eling with all required paperwork
Health issues - none
```

Behavior - sweet, loves everyone, gets along with other dogs
Housebroken - yes
Traveling with collar and leash. Crate not provided but please provide one if you wish
Reason for transport - Foster home to approved adoptive home

Friday, November 4
Denver,NC-High Point,NC
89 miles, 8:00-9:55pm/NEEDED

High Point,NC-Durham,NC
69 miles, 9:55-11:20pm/NEEDED

Durham,NC-South Hill,VA
72 miles, 1:20-1:00pm/NEEDED

South Hill,VA-Richmond,VA
82 miles, 1:00-2:40pm/NEEDED

Richmond,VA-Fredericksburg,VA
59 miles, 52:40-3:55pm/NEEDED

Fredericksburg,VA-Baltimore,MD
99 miles, 3:55-5:55pm/NEEDED

Baltimore,MD-Wilmington,DE
74 miles, 5:55-7:25pm/NEEDED

Overnight Needed in Wilmington, DE

Saturday, November 5
Wilmington,DE-Trenton,NJ
71 miles, 7:00-8:25am/NEEDED

Trenton,NJ-New Brunswick,NJ
36 miles, 8:25-9:25am/NEEDED

New Brunswick,NJ-Stamford,CT
74 miles, 9:25-11:25am/NEEDED

Stamford,CT-New Haven,CT
53 miles, 11:25-12:25pm/NEEDED

New Haven,CT-Hartford,CT
40 miles, 12:25-1:25pm/NEEDED

```
Hartford,CT-Southbridge,MA
52 miles,1:25-2:35pm/NEEDED

Southbridge,MA-Marlborough,MA
36 miles, 2:25-3:20pm/NEEDED

Marlborough,MA-Londonderry,NH
56 miles, 3:20-4:35pm
FILLED: adopter
```

I held my breath. Would anyone respond, or would all my behind-the-scenes coordinating producer work go down the drain? Even if the transport filled in time, would the people who volunteered to drive agree to let Sam and the other crew members point cameras at their faces, at Walker, and outside the windows as they drove?

As drivers started to trickle in and sign up for a few of the fifteen legs, I got an email from Terri, who was based in Ontario, Canada. The transport was nowhere near being filled and we were already at the point of having a Houston-sized problem.

"You've got to be kidding me," I replied with a frustrated sigh. Someone had informed Terri that our production crew was working undercover for the Massachusetts Department of Agricultural Resources, and that we had been enlisted to capture transporters on tape.

The rumors didn't stop there. I was also reported as being a firefighter posing as a producer. I had to laugh. At one hundred and fifteen pounds, I couldn't pull a fire hose if my life depended on it. Someone had me mixed up with someone else. After looking into it, there was indeed a female firefighter with the same name as mine, in close proximity to where I lived.

I understood Terri's point of view. She was, after all, based in Ontario. All she knew of this whole Massachusetts animal-profiling thing was what she saw coming across the message boards, and some of it was scary. And why would she ever want to chance allowing a rescued dog to be confiscated, possibly brought to a kill-shelter and, instead of going home, be twice burned?

I was concerned about the transport, too. We had been informed that a transport driver had been detained by Massachusetts Department of Agriculture personnel for hours while the animals on board and accompanying paperwork were scrutinized. The transporter was someone I had met and really liked. In fact, this person had driven Blondie part of the way to her adoptive home months before. Word had it that the driver was treated in a menacing and exceedingly impolite manner.

"What was the worst that could happen?" I mulled. One of our drivers could get pulled over with our fully vetted and health certified pup and then, yes! I would finally get my interview with the Department of Agriculture personnel!

At any rate, it was time to stop stressing and pull out the proofs. I sent Terri my bio information cluttered with productions, Bean Town-based institutions of higher learning I had attended, articles of mine that had been published, and pointy statues I had won.

With suspicions laid to rest and the investigation closed, Terri concentrated on doing what she does best. She posted her driver request again the following day, and on Wednesday, she also posted to another group.

```
[TRUCK-N-PAWS]
TRANS: Denver,NC - Londonderry,NH
November 4-5, 2005
Must Fill By Thurs.
```

By early Thursday morning, the transport looked like it would have to be cancelled. There were holes everywhere.

```
[OnTheRoadAgain] Need 7 Legs By This Afternoon
Nov. 4/5 Denver,NC - Londonderry,NH
```

Terri tried again, using a word reserved for very special situations.

```
[TRUCK-N-PAWS] URGENT: 6 Legs Needed By Today
Nov. 4-5 Denver,NC - Londonderry,NH
```

Later the same day, Terri emailed everyone with an update:

```
Hi Everyone: A decision will be made between
8 and 9 pm this evening about whether the
transport is a go. Please let me know if you
```

need to be phoned. This is an updated view of the transport. 5 Legs to Go!

CROSSPOST WIDELY: Transport leaves tomorrow morning so all legs must be filled by late this afternoon/early evening. Thanks to everyone who is crossposting!

Terri Epp
Leamington, Ontario, CANADA

Friday, November 4
Denver,NC-Mocksville,NC
48 miles/8:00-9:20am/Filled: Melanie

Mocksville,NC-Durham,NC
104 miles/9:20-11:20am/Filled: Alisa

Durham,NC-South Hill,VA
72 miles/1:20-1:00pm/NEEDED

South Hill,VA-Richmond,VA
82 miles/1:00-2:40pm/Filled: Jennifer

Richmond,VA-Fredericksburg,VA
59 miles/2:40-3:55pm/ Filled: Mary

Fredericksburg,VA-Laurel,MD
75 miles/3:55-5:40pm/NEEDED

Laurel,MD-Wilmington, DE
91 miles/5:55-7:35pm/Filled: Janet

Overnight Needed in Wilmington,DE/Filled: Sue

Saturday, November 5
Wilmington,DE-Trenton,NJ,
71 miles, 6:00-7:25am/NEEDED

Trenton,NJ-New Brunswick,NJ
36 miles/7:25-8:25am/Filled: Deette

New Brunswick,NJ-Stamford, CT
74 miles/8:25-10:25am/NEEDED

```
Stamford,CT-New Haven,CT
53 miles/10:25-11:25am/NEEDED

New Haven,CT-Hartford, CT
40 miles/11:25-12:25pm/Filled:Linda

Hartford,CT-Marlborough, MA
52 miles/12:25-2:10/ Filled:Jill

Marlborough,MA-Londonderry, NH
56 miles/2:10-3:25pm/Filled: adopter
```

It was Thursday night and we still had five missing legs. I was a wreck. I scrambled nervously through a host of producer details, just in case the transport miraculously filled.

Don Tate, our Associate Producer in Charlotte, would interview Janet, and then Melanie. He would tape Walker leaving with Melanie for the first leg of the trip. Another producer friend, John Hawkes, had agreed to spend the day with the adoptive family.

My production comrades and crew members were calling one by one. On-location production required lots of preparation. They needed information I still didn't have.

"Is this transport thing a go?" they asked. "Should we be firing up the batteries, or not?"

A half hour later, Terri emailed her team again.

```
The transport is a GO! I have one leg [New
Brunswick, NJ to Stamford, CT] to fill for
Saturday and I will be sure we have a driver.
There will be a few more updates to the over-
night, the last leg, and the missing leg as
soon as this information is available.

I would like all of tomorrow's drivers to con-
tact me once meeting spots are arranged.

Terri Epp
Leamington, Ontario, CANADA
```

Russ and I had dubbed Walker's transport "Wild Ride," and it would surely live up to its name. "The Wild Ride is on!" I told our crew excitedly, and early the next morning, with one leg still missing, the transport prepared for lift-off.

The next morning, November 4, at 6:43 a.m., just a little over an hour before Leg One would embark, a message appeared from Terri:

> I just wanted to let everyone know New
> Brunswick to Stamford is filled, and I will be
> in touch with the driver information. Happy
> transporting to all today. I know you will all
> be great :))
>
> Terri Epp
> Leamington, Ontario, CANADA

Though our circle of friends in the animal rescue and transport arena was widening, in some ways, it was getting smaller too. Little did Terri know that the person who had stepped up to save the transport was someone we had already met.

> Hi Bonnie: The person who is doing the last
> leg is part of a group that I recently joined
> called the Bunderground Railroad. This is a
> network of coordinators and drivers who trans-
> port rescued bunny rabbits. I don't know if you
> have time to give to the transport of small
> animals (other than dogs) but I think they
> would provide a very different perspective to
> the production.
>
> If interested, please contact Jennifer
> Barbieri.
>
> Thanks.
>
> Terri

Walker's Finalized Transport Schedule
Friday, November 4

Denver,NC-Mocksville,NC
48 miles/8:00-9:20am/Filled: Melanie

Mocksville,NC-Durham,NC
104 miles/9:20-11:20am/Filled: Alisa

Durham,NC-South Hill,VA
72 miles/11:20-1:00pm/Filled: Susie

South Hill,VA-Richmond,VA
82 miles/1:00-2:40pm/Filled: Jennifer S.

Richmond,VA-Fredericksburg,VA
59 miles/2:40-3:55pm/Filled: Mary

Fredericksburg,VA-Laurel,MD
75 miles/3:55-5:40pm/Filled: Jeri

Laurel,MD-Wilmington,DE
91 miles/5:40-7:35pm/Filled: Janet

Overnight Needed in Wilmington, DE: Filled: Sue

Saturday, November 5

Wilmington,DE-Trenton,NJ
71 miles/6:00-7:25am/Filled: Bob

Trenton,NJ-New Brunswick,NJ
36 miles/7:25-8:25am/Filled: Deette

New Brunswick,NJ-Stamford,CT
74 miles/8:25-10:25am/Filled: Jennifer B.

Stamford,CT-New Haven,CT
53 miles/10:25-11:25am/Filled: Rose

New Haven,CT-Hartford,CT
40 miles/11:25-12:25pm/Filled: Linda

Hartford,CT-Marlborough,MA
86 miles/12:25-2:10pm/Filled: Jill

```
Marlborough,MA-Londonderry,NH
56 miles/2:10-3:25pm/Filled: Amanda
```

```
Terri Epp
Leamington, Ontario, CANADA
```

Walker's journey had actually begun long before his scheduled transport to New England. When he was just a little pup, he was surrendered to a pound. He was both a black dog and a mixed breed, which meant he already had two strikes against him. Ending up in a kill pound was strike three.

> *We domesticated animals to be pets for us and I feel like we've kind of let them down if we let them get to the point where they are on death row. What has a dog done where he deserves to be on death row? To me, death row is just people's failure to provide for the dog or cat.*
>
> *We rescued Walker out of Lincoln County Pound when he was four weeks old. He's close to ten months right now so he definitely deserves this good home that he's going to. He's sweet, great with kids, other dogs, cats. I know whoever's getting him is getting just a really, really good dog.*
>
> *He's never gotten car sick, of course he's never really traveled this far…*
>
> *Sometimes you hate to see them go, especially when they've been with you for so long, but I had to be unselfish, I had to be realistic. I can't keep every dog or animal that I rescue or I'd have nine hundred back here, so I'm happy when they get their own family.*
>
> *Janet Northrop*

Terri stayed in touch with her drivers as the day marched on. Melanie had handed Walker off to Alisa, who was on her way to meet Susie.

Friday morning
I would like all of tomorrow's drivers to contact me once meeting spots are arranged. Please
call when your leg of the transport is complete. Be sure and have your cell phones on one
hour prior to the transport, bring along the
schedule, and have fresh drinking water for the
dog.

Thanks so much to all of you. Alisa and Susie
should just about be ready to meet in Durham.

Terri

Friday 11:46 am
The transport is running on schedule and Susie
is on her way to South Hill to meet Jennifer.

Terri

Friday 1:09 pm
The transport continues to run right on sched-
ule and Walker is with Jennifer on his way to
Richmond, VA.

Terri

Friday 3:57 pm
Mary just called and Walker is with Jeri and
heading for Laurel, MD. I guess he is a real
little gentleman and has been hamming for the
cameras :))

Terri

Friday 6:51 pm
Jeri called to say the meeting with Janet who
is on her way to Wilmington to meet Sue (the
overnight) went well and a bit ahead of sched-

ule. Walker is getting tired of traveling and is ready for a comfy bed and a nice overnight.

Walker en route.

I want to thank each and every person involved in today's trans-port. First of all I really appreci-ate so many people missing work and giving of their time on a week-day. The transport ran right on time and often ahead of schedule. Everyone called in to let me know how every-thing was going and how Walker was doing.

Walker rides!

I look forward to tomorrow's transport with a great group of drivers.

Terri

Sue, Al, and Marlee, who live with two Huskies, cared for Walker overnight. It was Bob's turn to drive the bewildered traveler early the next morning. Terri's communiqués continued.

Saturday 7:57 am
Bob called right on schedule to say Deette had left the Trenton area with Walker and was on her way to New Brunswick, NJ.

Terri

Saturday 9:12 am
The transport continues to run pretty much on
schedule.
Jennifer is on her way to Stamford, CT with
Walker.

Terri

Saturday 10:36 am
Rose has Walker and they are on their way to
New Haven, CT on schedule.

Terri

The trip was grueling for people on the production side of things. Sam rode with the transporters. I conducted interviews while Russ and our good friend Eric Pula met the hand-offs in the chase vehicle and taped other angles.

Once the transport arrived in New Haven, the production crew slowed things down for the rest of the day. It was impossible to keep it on schedule with all that the transporters wanted to say. They were opening up and beginning to share something of themselves, and I wanted to give them the time and the venue to be heard.

Our canine celebrity was walked, comforted, and offered water (sometimes with ice!) at every "changing of the driver." He had a look of perplexed delight about him as he met each new transporter and received special treats. Walker never got car sick, perhaps because he exercised at rest stops and did a lot of sleeping while on the road. When he wasn't asleep, he seemed genuinely interested in gazing out the windows, as everything was new.

There were four broadcast cameras focused on the pup and his adoptive family when they finally met at a large private parking lot. The mood was celebratory, and as Walker's new Dad lifted him up onto his van's seat, I heard him gently reassure the little black Aussie-mix who was once left for dead.

Walker's new dad, Carl.

Last car ride, I promise. Next one we'll go on vacation, but that won't be until next summer. All right, we're going home.

Carl Squatrito

I found Terri's last email after we had returned to our homestead by the sea.

Saturday 6:52 pm
Hi: I did hear from Jill that the pass off in MA went well and that Walker was on his way home. It sounds like some excellent footage and interviews took place.

I know some of you are camera shy so I wanted to especially thank you for allowing this transport to be filmed. I know Bonnie is happy too as this has been a long project in the making. Thanks to everyone who called in with reports and it sounds like Walker will make someone very happy.

Terri

I contemplated what we had witnessed over the past two days while we unpacked. People from two countries, virtual strangers, coming together and working as a team for the sake of one rescued animal. I pressed the play button and there they were – the volunteer transporters. RoseAnne had brought her baby, her mother, and young son so that they too could participate in saving the life of a dog. Linda was noticeably pregnant, and I thought I saw her crying as she handed Walker over to Jill.

Jill had a soothing voice and, prior to Walker, she had transported a paralyzed Dachshund who came with a wheelchair-type cart. Amanda, a first-timer, was astounded by the fluidity of the transport system, and she reveled in driving the last leg. I called Russ over, so he could see her dancing with Walker at a rest stop.

"All they needed was some good Polka music," I remarked before re-winding it to play it back again.

Exhausted, I still wanted to view John's tapes and see Walker's new home. With the footage in fast forward, I stopped when I saw a massive, colorful bird roaming around a large outdoor pen.

"Look Russ!" I said. "A turkey!" Soon some clucking chickens walked into view, then some quacking baby ducks. Then Carl. He walked over to the turkey (which some consider to be unattractive creatures), bent down slowly, and hugged him.

I had never seen anyone hug a turkey before. The turkey seemed to appreciate it, and sat contentedly on the ground while Carl stroked him on the back. What happened next took me by surprise, and I made a point of telling John about it.

Carl's young son, who must have been watching him out of frame, walked into the camera's eye. He picked up one of the wandering chickens ever so gently, and hugged her in exactly the same way as his father had hugged the turkey. Then he put her on the ground and stroked her back while whispering to her. His father looked on, and smiled.

Film and video footage is like that. It reveals poignant nuances about the human condition that don't require any dialogue to move us to tears. I sent a quick email off to Terri before allowing myself to collapse for the night.

```
Thanks for all your help and expertise Terri.
Walker was handed off to his adoptive fam-
ily with great fanfare. They are ecstatic and
in love with him. We're all so thrilled for
Walker. The transporters were so patient and
so wonderfully cooperative as we captured this
```

```
story in the making. We'll begin the prep. work
for your interview on Monday....

Take care,

Bonnie
```

Her usual humble self, Terri wouldn't take credit for her efforts.

```
Hi Bonnie: I am just happy I could be a small
part of this. Thank you for including me.

Terri
```

Trip Notes from the Transport Drivers

Thanks for the hard work everyone; it was great meeting you and knowing that Walker is going to an awesome home. I would be happy to help out again.

Melanie

...most people don't know that this "railroad" even exists; in fact I just found out a year ago. It's amazing and I'm so glad to be a part of it.

Deette

Oh, Walker was such a pleasure and a real gentleman! Thanks for the opportunity to participate. I hope he's home safe by now snuggling with his new family.

Linda

I just wanted to let you know it was a pleasure for me to take the last leg of this trip and help Walker and all out. He is such a sweet dog, and was so friendly. He looked very glad to see his new family – and his new family looked very glad to see him.

Amanda

I think he knew it was his last stop. We had his bed all ready for him, his bones, how could he not know?

Thank you so much everybody. We love Walker a lot, and we thank each and every one of you. He's here. He's here to stay.

Mary, Walker's new Mom

Working on the stairs.

So far it has been about twenty-four hours. Walker seems to be adjusting to no more car rides. He has a lot of puppy still in him.

I have to carry him up and down stairs. He must have no experience with stairs. That's okay, we can work on that.

He does show genuine affection. We love him already. He enjoys running without a leash, it's awesome to see him gallop puppy-like. I can see that he has some real speed that will develop.

Right now he is sacked out in our living room in front of an open fire in the fireplace. He is already very welcome and happy here.

Carl, Walker's new Dad

✦✦✦

And as for Checkers, the larger dog who appeared on the poster with Walker, he too went home soon afterward, and now resides quite regally in a place called Massachusetts.

Chapter Eleven
NEVER AGAIN

I spent a week in Gonzales, Louisiana with the HSUS... Rough. Heartbreaking. Maddening. Rewarding. The best time I have ever spent in hell. I am inexorably altered by my experiences.

Linda Rollins
Animal Rescue Volunteer

I wished I could have been there with Linda. Instead, while she was in hell, I was far away in a place that would have looked like heaven to any hurricane survivor.

I couldn't bear it, and started thinking about what we could do to help alleviate the suffering of people being hoisted up from rooftops. I made a list, and while checking the message boards, I came across a hurricane victim's plea for assistance.

A woman who had been relocated to Texas was distraught over her trapped animals. The dogs, a Pit Bull and a Lab-mix, were in St. Bernard Parish locked in a house. She begged on line for someone to please save her dogs, and to not be afraid of them – as they were surely hungry and scared.

I called her. The woman was worn out. She sounded lost, and almost lifeless. She had rented vehicles on two occasions to go back to her home, but was prevented from entering her neighborhood. I told her I would do whatever was necessary to convince someone to go and search for the dogs. With her address in hand, I looked on line for volunteers in her area. I called a woman named Kelsey, a rescuer with a boat.

Kelsey told me I was in the wrong area, and that Dr. White, a vet with the Iberia Humane Society could possibly help. Dr. White's harried assistant politely gave me instructions, things I would need to do before they could search for the dogs.

I called the woman in Texas and told her I would do the faxing and anything else required, she would just need to grant permission for Iberia Humane Society, Best Friends Animal Society, and Dr. Eric White to enter her house.

I raced to my attic and dragged the old fax machine out of its dusty box. It was gratifying to know that help would soon be on the way. I wanted desperately to aid this fellow citizen of mine, who was so obviously despondent and laden with grief.

The woman contacted me a little later in the day. The rescue team had gone into the house and found the dogs. Blue and Lucy were dead.

"My babies did not make it. Thank you for all your help and prayers," was all she had the strength to say.

"What will she do now?" I asked myself while sobbing over someone else's dogs. What exactly do people do when they have lost everything?

◆◆◆

Two months later, I met Linda on line. She was looking for a ride north for a Red Heeler named Winston. I gave her Terri Epp's contact information and, as we emailed back and forth, she shared her experiences in the hurricane-ravaged zone.

> We all took on "pet" (pardon the pun) projects that humanized the inhumanity of the thousands of suffering animals that we cared for. Mine was a non-descript little male tabby kitten in ICU.
>
> He looked just like a special needs kitten that I have at home. He's the one that made me say, "I'll take him home with me if he lives." He was about ten weeks old. I persuaded the VMAT (Veterinary Medical Assistance Teams) vets to give him a transfusion, then another one

later on that night. I tucked him in around midnight, and at 6 a.m., went back to check on him before we made the forbidden run for coffee. He was sleeping and breathing quietly.

Linda loses the kitten.

Twenty minutes later, we returned, and he was dead. Freshly dead. Still very warm. I cradled him in my arms and cried like a baby. Totally lost it over that little guy. I felt soooo guilty that I wasn't there to hold him as he left.

As I write this, tears fall like it was yesterday. The picture of me holding him appeared on the front page of my local newspaper, in full color.

It triggered an outpouring of kindness from strangers that left me (even more) stunned. An eighty-four-year-old woman shut-in called, crying, asking me where she could send money. Cards from people I've never met arrived in my mailbox. Amazing.

Linda posted her struggle with trauma-induced stress in hopes of helping volunteers who went south and were still suffering from the experience.

I spent a year in Gonzales the last week of September. (That's what it felt like.)

I too have been inexorably altered, and now, four weeks and one day after my return, am coping…barely. I got home on Tuesday, 10.4, and by Friday, 10.7 had found myself a trauma therapist.

*I stayed in for a week, crying every day. I had the barking in my head for two weeks. What has helped me, so far, is staying in touch, staying involved, and devoting myself to the continued belief that one person **can** make a huge difference. **And we did. Each one of us!***

*I felt underutilized for half a second, then saw that there was **always** a need for **something**. I* *immersed myself in the ICU, doing nursing sixteen hours a day.*

I cried a lot, but when the tears began to flow, I looked at the poor burned, maimed, starving, desperate faces all around me who still managed a weak tail wag, or the cats who would finally rub their head against your hand, after all the injustices they had suffered (you know how cats take everything so personally!) or finally taken a bite of food on their own, or peed or pooped, and it made my despair insignificant and surmountable.

The hardest thing I ever did was leave on the 4th. I have been wracked with guilt for leaving before the end, but I now realize that we are not even close to "the end," even though Lamar closed on the 15th.

*Celebrate the lives you touched, and saved, and know that the ones who died in our care, **died in our care**, with our love, and with a gentle hand on their heads and a full belly. We did the very best we could.*

Linda Rollins
Animal Rescue Volunteer

I got to the end of the email and for some reason, I had drifted back to Salem State College. Jane Goodall was at the podium. Her words, delivered with all of the wisdom and optimism she carried with her, pulsated like a beacon in my brain.

Every individual matters.
Every individual has a role to play.
Every individual makes a difference.

Jane Goodall

♦♦♦

My hurricane-related news arrived daily through Best Friends Animal Society, Eric Rice's Dog Blog, and various message groups containing endless lists of what individual parishes needed, and specific guidelines for mailing goods to them.

Eric Rice called me a couple of times late at night, all fatigued. I could practically feel him sweating through the phone in the ever-present stickiness of post-Katrina New Orleans. He and his friend Lisa had been called to rescue a small dog locked in a bathroom, and they decided to bring a camera along. Lisa sent me the footage.

Eric called to the little dog from atop a rickety ladder, not knowing if the animal was still alive. "Hey little guy!" he yelled up in a tone that seemed to say, "Your nightmare's over, we've come for you." Eric then prefaced the rescue attempt for his audience.

"Where is he? I can't even tell you how bad it smells in there and what this poor dog has to live in, but I'm gonna go in and get him out. These animals want out of these houses so bad!"

The camera was all over the dark, filthy bathroom and then Eric's voice returned. "He's trying to climb up the wall! He's a Pit Bull, he's not gonna bite, here he comes!"

I was jubilant as a woman grabbed the dog securely and lifted her up (yes, a little girl!) over the bathroom windowsill and down the ladder. "How many days after the storm?" Eric asked the woman while gasping for clean air.

"Tomorrow will be thirty," she replied as she offered the skin and bones dog some water.

"That's probably the fifth dog that we've pulled out thirty days after the storm, just our little group in the last two or three days," Eric said for the camera.

He repeated himself as if he couldn't believe his eyes. "That's almost thirty days locked in a bathroom. Thirty days locked in a bathroom right here."

✦✦✦

I heard about another woman named Jane through Denise DeVynck, who had coordinated the transport for Bailey, the senior Miniature Poodle. Like Jane Goodall, this Jane wasn't afraid to break with tradition when something needed to be done.

I decided to help animals in desperate situations back in 1995. I went to check on some elephants at a circus for a friend. When I arrived at the circus, I saw five Asian elephants chained by one front leg and one back leg unable to take even a step in either direction. It was over ninety degrees and they had absolutely no access to shade or water.

Truly, these animals were in a desperate situation and I vowed to educate people about the abuse of elephants (and all exotic animals) in circuses. Of course, my work for elephants led me to other ways to help animals, including becoming certified to help animals in disasters. After my certification, I rescued animals from floods and tornados.

Every time I hear of any natural disaster I always think about the animals…Hurricane Katrina was no different. However, when my mother called me in tears and said they were forcing people to leave their animals trapped in their homes, on rooftops, and on the streets, I knew I had to get to New Orleans to help.

I, along with hundreds of volunteers from all over the world, went through the city by foot and by boat searching for the animals who were trapped and stranded. In the beginning I would yell to dogs and would use their barking as a guide. Sadly, the animals were everywhere. We truly could not break into the homes and rescue the animals fast enough…that was the most frustrating part.

Once we rescued an animal, we would spray paint the house with the date and the animal who was removed, and bring the animal to the temporary shelter we had set up one hour away from New Orleans.

Some animals knew they were being rescued and others were just terrified. I had animals who were stuck on rooftops or inside flooded houses who literally jumped into my arms and licked my face. However, there were other animals who were just so traumatized and did not realize I was trying to help them.

The animals had been through so much, considering they endured two hurricanes, flooding, and the evacuation of the entire city around them! Certainly, anyone can understand why they were so frightened.

It is very difficult for all the animal rescue volunteers to cope with what we saw in New Orleans. We saw animals who died while hiding under the covers of the bed they once shared with their human companion. We saw dogs who drowned because people left them chained outside. We saw dogs who desperately scratched at their front door to escape.

These memories are haunting, but the worst memories are the dead animals I saw who lived through the two hurricanes and the flooding only to die of dehydration, or starvation, because there were not enough people to get to them in time.

In my opinion, that is the greatest tragedy of all. With all the money that was pouring in to help animals, there should have been an army of animal rescue people.

I have been able to deal with those images by trying to offset them with images of the over thirteen hundred animals I carried to safety. I try to focus on the sweet faces who would not have lived if I had not been there to save them.

I can't even imagine what the people who were told to evacuate without their animals have endured emotionally. These people trusted the government agencies that told them that they would be able to return in two days. I can't even imagine the frustration they felt when they were not able to return for seven weeks.

I have spoken with many, many people in New Orleans who carry so much guilt for leaving their animals behind. But it was not their fault.

Most people were forced (some at gunpoint) to leave their animals when they were being rescued by boat or by helicopter. Sadly, many of the people who died are those who refused to leave their animals behind.

The most tragic part of this entire situation for animals is that it was preventable. People should have been encouraged to take their animals with them…not leave them behind.

Everyone who spent time in New Orleans and the Gulf Coast has been transformed. We are all part of a club whose common ground is the sadness and death we experienced. We will never forget the sights, sounds, and smells of that time.

The rescue mission became very difficult when the media showed less interest and people around the country thought that everything in New Orleans was "back to normal." We rescued animals out of homes for nine weeks after the hurricane!

When the media attention died, it was very difficult to get volunteers to come to New Orleans. When windows and doors blew open, thousands of animals left their homes in search of food and water. In addition to the animals who were still in homes and barely alive, there were thousands of animals on the streets who needed help.

I decided to keep rescuing in that region when the larger animal rescue groups left for one reason and one reason only…the animals. There were clearly more animals locked inside homes and lost on the streets that I could not and would not just leave to die.

I was thrilled that volunteers coordinated transports of rescued animals! Without these transports we never would have been able to rescue as many animals as we did. Each transport opened up space at the temporary shelter for us to rescue more animals.

In the three months after the national groups had left the area, we rescued over two thousand animals. These are animals who would have died of dehydration and starvation if we did not make the decision to stay and rescue them. Almost six months after the hurricane, we were still rescuing animals off the streets and reuniting them with their families.

The most important change that must be implemented in hurricane-affected regions to make life better for animals is a firm policy/law that animals must be evacuated when humans evacuate.

The national animal protection organizations, that raised millions and millions of dollars through this disaster, must work hard to see that legislation is passed that includes animals in evacuation plans. People must lobby their legislators and urge them to support legislation to include animals in disaster evacuation plans. In addition, as individuals, people must never leave their animals behind when evacuating...my motto is "If I leave, they leave."

Jane Garrison
Founder, Animal Rescue New Orleans

Russ and I interviewed Kara Peterson and Cynthia Sweet upon Cynthia's return from Louisiana.

We decided to focus Project Starfish right away on helping the animals in Louisiana, right in the aftermath of Hurricane Katrina. The reason that we hope we can continue to exist is because their problems are not going to go away as Hurricane Katrina floodwaters recede.

Kara Peterson
Project Starfish

I don't feel like it had anything to do with people wanting to abandon their animals. I think people were under the assumption that they would be gone for a couple of days.

Cynthia Sweet
Project Starfish

The two Massachusetts-based women were unstoppable, despite the fact that hurricane-affected animals weren't being welcomed into their state. Though residents came forth by the thousands offering to foster displaced dogs and cats, the state's red tape and isolation compliance requirements served as a major roadblock.

With not enough time to clear the hurdles set up for them in advance, the women opted to work with more flexible states. They made arrangements for Katrina's four-legged survivors to be transported to Vermont and Pennsylvania, where they were greeted with open arms.

◆◆◆

Animal Ark, a no-kill shelter in Minnesota, is another organization that came to the rescue of animal victims in the hurricane-affected areas. Animal Ark's Executive Director Mike Fry conveyed that his staff and volunteers logged about 8,000 hours in the hurricane zone helping animals. They took 250 animals back to Minnesota and cared for them while they worked to find the families of the displaced pets.

Mike took in a little Katrina rescue named Goldie. After Goldie was returned to his family, Mike posted the following on Animal Ark's daily blog.

```
10/26/2005 - To David and Goldie, aka Tiny
Posted From Animal Ark Shelter - Minnesota
Posted by Mike Fry

This morning, I started my day by talking with
Goldie's mom. It was one of the most difficult
phone conversations I have had in my life. But,
being on the phone was nothing compared to the
horror she and her family are living.

Her son, David, had been Goldie's "dad".
David loved Goldie, and two other dogs that
lived with Goldie, whose real name turned out
to be Tiny.

Tiny is a Pomeranian/Chihuahua mix who came to
live at my house in the wake of Hurricane Ka-
trina. Of the hundreds of animals we have res-
```

cued, his is also the first story that I know in its entirety, thanks to the time spent talking to David's mom on the phone this morning.

David, I am sure, would have told me the story, but he is no longer alive to tell his or Tiny's tale. I feel comfortable in "knowing" this, because after hearing his story, I feel bonded to him, and I feel like I know him. Our lives are connected through the life of a little dog that we both love.

Goldie aka Tiny.

David lived in St. Bernard Parish, a neighborhood in New Orleans that was hit very hard when the levy broke during the storm. He shared his home with his daughters and his three dogs. The dogs were spoiled and even slept in bed with him at night.

When the levy broke, he and the daughters were home. They survived by climbing the stairs in their home, going to the second floor, and ultimately, into the attic. As water engulfed the interior of their home, they raced to save each other and the dogs.

Trapped in the attic, their only route to safety was to dig a hole in the roof of the home from the inside. They lived on top of the house with the three dogs for days awaiting rescue.

Eventually, a small boat came by. With it came good news: a larger boat was coming to the levy wall to pick people up and take them to safety. So the family and the dogs boarded the boat and headed for the levy. They lived on the levy with several other people and some other pets for days with no food or shelter.

They watched helplessly as some of the other humans and pets died in the heat. Eventually, a boat did come, but the news was not good. Tiny and the other pets were not allowed.

In desperation, David took a small row boat into St. Bernard Parish and found an apartment building where he could leave the dogs. The third floor apartment had nearly three feet of water in it. By piling furniture and mattresses in the living room, he created a dry island the dogs could survive on. He left them with food and water; then he and his daughters evacuated to safety.

Tiny and his canine friends were rescued 10 days later and taken to Tylertown, Mississippi. Tiny eventually found his way to my home in Minnesota.

But, life for David was not as happy. He and his family searched night and day to locate his lost pets. Struggling with the loss of his home and property, and unable to locate his beloved dogs, he hanged himself from an oak tree at his mother's house.

His mom swears that had David been allowed to evacuate with his dogs, he would be alive today. Following his death, his mother continued the search for the missing dogs. With the help of Best Friends Animal Society, we were connected to Tiny and David's mom and the story is complete.

I thanked David's mom for sharing his story. I asked her to give Tiny a big hug and kiss for me. I hung up the phone. . . and I cried, not just for David and Tiny, but for all the families and all of the pets that were put through

unnecessary hell due to crazy FEMA and Red
Cross policies.

Hurricane Katrina was a natural disaster - but
the real devastation inflicted on these families came about because of human choices. If
we are to call ourselves a civilized nation,
we must swear to never do anything like this
again.

Following the Gulf Coast catastrophe, Congressman Tom
Lantos (D-CA) and his co-sponsors Christopher Shays (R-CT),
Don Young (R-AK), James Oberstar (D-MN), and Barney Frank
(D-MA) introduced legislation to guarantee that in future disasters,
people will not be forced to abandon their household pets.

The Pets Evacuation and Transportation Standards Act of
2005 (PETS Act, H.R. 3858), requires local and state emergency
preparedness authorities to include in their evacuation plans the
means to accommodate household pets and service animals in case
of a disaster. Local and state authorities would be required to submit
their compliance plans in order to qualify for grants from the Federal
Emergency Management Agency.

The Senate version of the PETS Act (S. 2548) gives FEMA
the authority to assist in developing these plans. It also requires the
provision of essential assistance for people with household pets and
service animals, and for the animals themselves, following a major disaster and authorizes funds to help states create emergency shelters
for people accompanied by their animals.

Chapter Twelve
THE CURE

The day was all sunlit and blustery – the perfect background for our last location shoot. We soon had every scene we needed for our follow-up segment to Walker's journey home.

Russ gave me a look of relief knowing this project, the one he'd been so very faithful to, had finally wrapped production. I looked away, and a strange sort of heaviness weighed into my bliss. I recognized it as I watched a once abandoned and doomed pound puppy make a happy dash for his ball. The turbulence continued until it permeated every unoccupied space in my soul.

"Aren't they all deserving?" begged the interrogator in my mind. "Isn't every homeless animal worthy of the warm and caring embrace that Walker received?"

It was the end of a very special journey for Walker and for me, and it pained me to hear his one last bark good-bye. As I hopped up into the equipment truck, I offered my final wave to this joy-filled adopted dog and his family.

♦♦♦

At the close of each interview we conducted during our production phase, individuals were asked to share their ideas for a solution to our unwanted-animal problem. The words from some of the people I've come to know and love are with me still. They are far more meaningful now than they were at the beginning of this adventure, and I understand why.

It's because I've looked into these animals' aching eyes. I've heard whimpers echo off of cold, cruel cement walls, and I've reached in between bars to hold paws gently in my hand. I've seen animals plead

for liberty and affection, and yes, I know beyond a shadow of a doubt that animals have feelings, despite what the most scholarly among us may say.

As I turn the pages in my notebook where people contemplate a cure, I can recall every homeless animal we've encountered along the way. All of their faces come rushing to the forefront of my memory, then silently disappear.

Worth saving?

Tragically, over five million friendly, loving dogs and cats are killed every year because there are not enough homes for them. The best thing that people can do to eliminate this killing is to spay/neuter your animals and only adopt animals from shelters or online rescue sites like 1-800-Save-A-Pet.com or Petfinder.com.

Jane Garrison
Animal Rescue New Orleans

If we can get access to free sterilization for cats and dogs, I think that our unwanted pet problem will go down substantially. That's the easy fix. The harder fix is to address owner responsibility. When you decide to be a guardian or an owner of a cat, there's a lifelong responsibility and a financial responsibility.

Stacy LeBaron
Merrimack River Feline Rescue Society

Big dogs have twelve and thirteen puppies in a litter. Those twelve and thirteen puppies have twelve and thirteen puppies. It's just staggering, so we need to spay and neuter...

Lorraine Ehrhart
Miami-Dade Rescue Railroad

I like to work on things that will totally change the landscape. Until we do that we are going to have these problems of overpopulation and abuse.

We need a new generation of people who treat animals differently. I hate to be skeptical but I see this evolving over a few hundred years, not ten or twenty.

Eric Rice
Animal Rescue Volunteer

The biggest thing that individuals can do to help the homeless animal problem is to take care of their pets and have them spayed and neutered at an early age, and consider adopting from a local shelter.

Kevin Boyle
Volunteer Pilot

I feel that we in Massachusetts have a moral and ethical responsibility to care for animals, wherever they are.

The animals in the south and in many other parts of the country — they face problems that should not be faced in a country with the resources that we have and as many animal lovers as we have.

So we hope to really focus on education and action, and keeping the distance between the person who wants to help, and the animal who needs help, to a minimum.

Kara Peterson, Co-Founder
Project Starfish

I think animals, if you look in the news (especially dogs), they do a lot of service for people, and I think we owe a service to them, to try to do what we can to make sure they don't end up on a cold, damp pound floor just to be euthanized in three or four days.

They're all deserving, and they all have their ways of touching our lives and they deserve our help; and I want to be that person or at least one of those people…

Janet Northrop
4 Paws Animal Rescue

Sadly, we are not at a point in history where we know how our nation's homeless animal crisis will be resolved, or if we do, we are not ready, willing, or able to end it.

Despite all that, something about whatever emanates from inside the volunteer animal transporters gives me a glimmer of hope. Something tells me that this journey will soon be repeated millions of times over, though the names, places, and circumstances will change.

Let's pray it won't be long before we can re-tell Walker's story for every homeless animal who still waits for a ride to freedom.

"Dog Transport" by Marlee Zabriskie

Epilogue

We began the labor-intensive, brain-burning task of editing the project on a windy afternoon in September.

Everyone who edits film, video, or digital media does so in their own particular and sometimes peculiar way. These days, technological aids make the process easier and more fluid, sometimes even fun.

I chose to edit our reality-based docu-drama the hard way. First I watched all of the footage, endless hours of it, at least a few times. Then I transcribed the dialogue that I thought was usable and committed much of it to memory.

The people talking got carried around with me everywhere I went, until I knew them very well. I replayed their stories in my head over and over, rearranging them until they looked and sounded comfortable beside each other, like they were meant to be together. Then we got out the fancy editing equipment and married people at the seams.

Throughout the initial stages of editing, I was in turmoil. With the finite number of minutes and seconds afforded us to tell a story, each person's departure from the screen felt too soon, and left me wanting to linger with them longer. I wanted to give Lorraine the chance to talk about the dog who inspired her mission, and the pact she made with God, but there wasn't time. I wished Debbie could have shared her day-to-day joys caring for tiny, blessed little dogs, but the clock was ticking. I would have liked to include rescued dogs from Georgia jumping all over Gayle as she laughed out loud and ushered them to a better life, but it just didn't work out.

Russ had his own wish list. He would have liked to include other modes of animal transport – via canoe, railways, snowmobiles, motor cycles. He had asked me to set up location shoots for people transporting out-of-time horses, emus, cows, and, "Couldn't we find anyone needing to move a giraffe from one sanctuary to another?"

When Russ had finished editing the drivers, he let me have a look. "Okay," I said excitedly after seeing the transport network in action, "let's get the rest of these people in there."

When all was said and done, I likened the production to a dance. Everyone was properly positioned, and when the music started, each person took someone else's hand. Ever so gently, politely, a member took a step forward, then bowed to the next person who would take center stage.

In the background there was carefully synchronized and lovingly executed movement as animals were whisked away in peoples' arms – quickly, quietly, from dark places to where they could see bright lights, and feel warmth again. The choreographer worked from a distance, unseen, yet enormously busy, aware of every misstep and leap of faith.

It was a sight to behold, a thing of rare beauty, and like an audience member at the close of a magnificent ballet, I gave the ensemble a standing ovation when the last leg was finally at rest. The group didn't wait for applause but hurried off to another performance, because animals were waiting and they had very little time. One of the dancers turned around, and though she was far away, I could see she was making an appeal to the audience. "There aren't enough players to carry them all," she said with her hand stretched forth. "Would anyone like to step up and join me for this dance?"

I pressed the eject button, reached into my pocket, and tossed the tiny jar of skepticism into the trash receptacle. In its place I put the project, where it would be safe until it was passed off to broadcast executives.

"What happens next is out of my hands," I reminded myself. Other people in high places would be making the decision as to whether our story was of sufficient social significance to share with the public at large. "I hope they all have dogs or cats," I said to Winky, the little Beagle-mix who was running around in circles at my feet. She stopped and looked at me, as if she was waiting for me to get on with the show.

"Alright, let's go to the park!" I said cheerily to my four-legged friend. Winky barked in agreement, spun around twice, then offered me her paw, just like she always does when she's experiencing an emotion widely recognized as happiness.

Acknowledgments

Special thanks to my "forever friends" Donald Tate, Sam Patton, Eric Pula, and Amanda MacFadgen for giving of themselves so that more animals could have a second chance.

Thanks to industry friends Pepper Lindsey and her kind-hearted, personable partner Kent. I appreciate Gay Schonbrunn for giving me a wide-open window on the world of animal rescue and transport.

My gratitude goes out to Katia Grossman and Kelly Sperber, both of whom reached out generously to a stranger. Thanks also to the handful of transporters who willingly made room in their lives and their vehicles for some storytellers.

My appreciation goes out to Tufts University professor Lisa Brukilaccio for daring to look deeper into the human-animal bond, and for encouraging me in my thinking. And special thanks to the late Chuck Howard, who had the greatest capacity for compassion of any human being I have ever known, and who showed me that all I had to do when I felt most defeated was "try another way."

Lastly, I must thank the animals I met and fell in love with, every one of them, including little Blondie, who fixed her eyes on mine and lassoed my heart.

Like Dorothy, when her house stopped spinning as she landed in Oz, I got caught up in a whirlwind and ended up someplace I didn't even know existed. I'm grateful for the chance given to me to be tossed about, shaken up, and transformed.

Thanks to all of you who chose to go with me, and to all of you who welcomed me aboard. I wouldn't have missed this ride for the world.

Meet Me in Cyberspace

If you would like to become involved in animal rescue and transport, please visit the web sites listed below. Volunteers like the people profiled in *Fifteen Legs* will help you connect with groups in your area. Many more volunteers are needed to escort rescued animals home.

almosthomerescue.org
animalarkshelter.org
animalrescueneworleans.org
bestfriends.org
bundergroundrailroad.org

canadianyorkshireterrierrescue.com
dawgsntexas.com
ericsdogblog.com
flyingpaws.org
4pawsanimalrescue.com

heartlandrabbitrescue.org
hsus.org
karmarescue.org
mdrr.org
mainecoonrescue.com

mrfrs.org
projectstarfish.org
puppymillrescue.com
saveadogandkids.org
spinrescue.org

trucknpaws.org
wildheartranch.org
groups.yahoo.com/group/I-40_Rescue_and_Transport/
groups.yahoo.com/group/OklahomaAnimalRescue/
groups.yahoo.com/group/OnTheRoadAgain/

Photo Credits

|

CHAPTER SEVEN

Betty (3)	Debbie Fahrenholtz
Puppy Miles	Sandy Clabaugh
Happy Miles	Sandy Clabaugh

CHAPTER EIGHT

Ms. Betty (2)	Debbie Fahrenholtz
Buck – a cruelty case (2)	courtesy Rutherford County Animal Control Facility
Buck running at the dog park	Holly and David Thomas
Buck at his forever home	Holly and David Thomas

CHAPTER NINE

Noelle before	courtesy MDRR** and Barbara Arco
Noelle during	courtesy MDRR** and Barbara Arco
And Noelle after treatment	courtesy MDRR** and Barbara Arco

CHAPTER TEN

Walker en route	(video source footage)
Walker rides	(video source footage)
Walker's new dad, Carl	(video source footage)
Working on the stairs	(video source footage)

CHAPTER ELEVEN

| Linda loses the kitten | Karen Hathaway |
| Goldie aka Tiny | Mike Fry |

CHAPTER TWELVE

| Worth saving? | Heidi Ott |

*RW BGRR is RabbitWise's Bunderground Railroad
**MDRR is Miami-Dade Rescue Railroad